# A CITIZEN'S GUIDE
# TO TERRORISM AND
# COUNTERTERRORISM

This *Citizen's Guide* addresses the public policy issues of terrorism and counterterrorism in the United States after bin Laden's death. Written for the thinking citizen and student alike, this succinct and up-to-date book takes a "grand strategy" approach toward terrorism and uses examples and issues drawn from present-day perpetrators and actors.

Christopher Harmon, a veteran academic of military theory who has also instructed U.S. and foreign military officers, organizes his book into three main sections. He first introduces the problem of America's continued vulnerability to terrorist attack by reviewing the long line of recent attacks and attempts against the United States, focusing specifically on New York City. Part II examines the varied ways in which the United States is already fighting terrorism, highlighting the labors of diverse experts, government offices, intelligence and military personnel, and foreign allies. The book outlines the various aspects of the U.S. strategy, including intelligence, diplomacy, public diplomacy, economic counterterrorism, and law and law-making. Next, in Part III, Harmon sketches the prospects for further action, steering clear of simple partisanship and instead listing recommendations with pros and cons, and also including factual stories of how individual citizens have made a difference in the national effort against terrorism. The final pages list further reading resources.

This slim book will contribute to our understanding of the problems surrounding terrorism and counterterrorism—and the approaches the United States may take to meet them—in the early 21st century.

**Christopher C. Harmon** is Horner Chair of Military Theory at Marine Corps University.

# CITIZEN GUIDES TO POLITICS AND PUBLIC AFFAIRS

Morgan Marietta and Bert Rockman, Series Editors

Each book in this series is framed around a significant but not well-understood subject that is integral to citizens'—both students and the general public—full understanding of politics and participation in public affairs. In accessible language, these titles provide readers with the tools for understanding the root issues in political life. Individual volumes are brief and engaging, written in short, readable chapters without extensive citations or footnoting. Together they are part of an essential library to equip us all for fuller engagement with the issues of our times.

### Titles in the series:

# A CITIZEN'S GUIDE TO TERRORISM AND COUNTERTERRORISM

*Christopher C. Harmon*

Routledge
Taylor & Francis Group
NEW YORK AND LONDON

First published 2014
by Routledge
711 Third Avenue, New York, NY 10017

and by Routledge
2 Park Square, Milton Park, Abingdon, Oxon OX14 4RN

*Routledge is an imprint of the Taylor & Francis Group, an informa business*

© 2014 Taylor & Francis

*Library of Congress Cataloging in Publication Data*
Harmon, Christopher C.
    A citizen's guide to terrorism and counterterrorism / Christopher C. Harmon. – First edition.
    pages cm – (Citizen guides to politics and public affairs)
    1. Terrorism–United States. 2. Terrorism–United States–Prevention. 3. Security, National–United States. I. Title.
    HV6432.H3776 2013
    363.325–dc23
    2013027918

ISBN: 978-0-415-70941-5 (hbk)
ISBN: 978-0-415-70942-2 (pbk)
ISBN: 978-1-315-88409-7 (ebk)

Typeset in Garamond
by EvS Communication Networx, Inc.

Printed and bound in the United States of America by Publishers Graphics, LLC on sustainably sourced paper.

This book for the citizens of the United States
is made possible by the generosity of Thomas Saunders,
his wife Jordan, daughter of
Major General Matthew C. Horner,
United States Marine Corps, and
the Marine Corps University Foundation.

# CONTENTS

CONTENTS

*Educate and inform ... the people. Enable them to see that it is their interest to preserve peace and order and they will preserve them.*

(Thomas Jefferson, letter to James Madison, 1787)

*Aggression must be judged, not from the standpoint of Right and Left, but of right and wrong .... We are in the midst of danger so great ... we are the guardians of causes so precious to the world ... .*

(Winston S. Churchill, Paris, 1936)

# SERIES FOREWORD

The reality of contemporary terrorism—no longer unique events, no longer unexpected except for the exact time and place—presents grave threats to the security and ideals of a free society. Coming to grips with those threats is the purpose of this volume in the Citizen's Guide series. Like each of our books, it is written for a general audience of citizens and students, addressing pressing problems with clear explanations. For this topic we turned to Christopher C. Harmon, a distinguished scholar at the Marine Corps University in Quantico, Virginia. Dr. Harmon holds the Major General Matthew C. Horner Chair in Military Theory and has written or edited previous books on understanding and combating modern terror, including the popular textbook *Terrorism Today* (now in its second edition). He has devoted his career to teaching the strategy and tactics of counterterrorism to military officers, civil servants, and diplomats, and he has been a pioneer in the study of how terrorist groups end. In this volume, Harmon addresses in clear and uncompromising language the most pressing questions many Americans have in the post-9/11 world of shocking violence from unfamiliar quarters: *Who is this enemy? Why are they doing this? Is it likely to continue?* And perhaps most importantly: *What can be done about it?*

Harmon addresses not only the nature of terrorism, but also the ongoing American grand strategy against it—a grand strategy that has far more than military elements. His book is about counterterrorism as much as terrorism itself. In order to see what must be done, we must understand terror's motivations and goals; we must comprehend the beliefs that inspire it and the world it wishes to create. This is the case because terrorism is not merely violence for the cameras, but violence for the political purposes promoted by that display. Harmon allows us to understand the nature of terrorist movements—guided by beliefs about the current world and visions of a future one—rather than seeing only random or incomprehensible acts. With that understanding we can see the true nature of the challenges we face and the possible roads ahead. With that hope we present this *Citizen's Guide to Terrorism and Counterterrorism*.

Morgan Marietta and Bert Rockman
*Series Editors*

# PREFACE

Three decades as public servant and graduate school professor have allowed me steady professional interaction with Americans about problems of terrorism and counterterrorism. It was sometimes difficult in years past for all of us to agree to the need to forcefully and consistently resist this modern scourge: terrorism. But its nature has been more apparent—and more lethal and ugly—since September 11, 2001. Our hardest challenges now are to understand terrorism well, including its newest forms, and to make our ongoing campaign against Al Qaeda, its allies, and its future variants a long-term success.

John Malkovich is an example of a citizen who sees the nature of terrorism clearly. When he directed his intriguing movie *The Dancer Upstairs* (2003) about a policeman hunting for the leader of Shining Path terrorists in Peru, he was challenged by a few who perceived the film to display anti-terrorist political prejudice. The film director's reply, in an interview, showed a principled understanding of why everyone should be against terrorism. Malkovich refuted the common phrase "One man's terrorist is another man's freedom fighter," calling that idea "utterly facile and idiotic, and actually obscene." He said the way in which ideology and terrorism combine makes our world brood under "the imminent threat of violence." "Every day, somewhere in the world, terrorists will murder people who have nothing to do with their cause, to promote their cause, and that's something the world is starting to grapple with now ... . [Terrorists] have their little causes, whatever they are. And one has to care about them profoundly or one is a target."[i]

These thoughtful replies by a man known mainly as an actor point to a general improvement in resolution in the moral picture of terrorism. It is encouraging to see so much common sense and clear thought in a public figure.

More formally, we have a superb definition of terrorism, produced in 1979 by a think tank called the Jonathan Institute and never surpassed for clarity: "Terrorism is the deliberate and systematic murder, maiming, and menacing of the innocent to inspire fear for political ends."

But that clear conception only takes us so far, and as citizens we remain troubled by many questions. *What is this enemy? How much does Al Qaeda matter given that Osama bin Laden is now dead? What other forms of terrorism still threaten? How is the United States fighting back? Do we have a coherent strategy? If so, do its parts fit together, as the many parts of a grand strategy should? How will Al Qaeda end? Will we be able to defeat terrorism in general?* The pages that follow are designed to help an informed public answer these questions, because it is we who are reflecting on, paying for, and participating in our global counterterrorist efforts.

For the many interviews and discussions behind these slender chapters, I am especially grateful to many citizens. They begin, of course, with my extended family, as well as Patrick McDonald, Jessica Groves, Jim Phillips, J. Q. Roberts, James Anderson, Michael Cooper, John Lenczowski, Paul Guppy, and Carl Shelton. Thanks are due to Audrey Hudgins and Eric Farquharson; it was their Seattle University-based, national award-winning Reserve Officer Training Corps program that provided the hospitable environment for the birth of this unique little book. Stase Rodebaugh of the Marine Corps University's writing center has given the work a proofing, though I remain responsible for any errors. John Hales of the Marine Corps University Foundation, my friend Kevin Smith, Charles R. Harmon, and Darren Fazzino and others have surveyed the last draft. Now, in June 2013, it may be worthy to become part of the Routledge Citizen's Guide series, well conceived and edited by Morgan Marietta and Bert Rockman.

Christopher C. Harmon

## Note

i "Interview with John Malkovich" by A.V. Club, May 7, 2003, www.avclub. com/articles/john-malkovich,13810/, accessed April 4, 2011.

# Part I

# THE THREAT

# 1

# WE AMERICANS REMAIN VULNERABLE TO TERRORIST ATTACK

Expecting to kill at least 40 people with his home-made car bomb, Faisal Shahzad parked it in Times Square, New York City, and returned to his home in Connecticut. With the calculation characteristic of a terrorist, he had monitored live video feeds over the Internet for three months, studying the square to decide when and where to position the car bomb in order to kill the most Americans.

On May 1, 2010, his cold-blooded work seemed all done. He logged onto his home computer to contact his handlers in the Pakistani Taliban.[1] They had helped to plan and finance the attack, and stayed in touch with Shahzad via a special software program that had been installed in his computer during his training. With the bomb in place, it remained only to await results. The defendant later admitted he had planned to commit a further attack two weeks later, also in New York City. He would continue, he said, until capture or death.[2] But New York street vendor Duane Jackson saw smoke emitting from the terrorist's bomb-laden SUV. Jackson alerted police—a tribute to the city's ongoing "If you see something, say something" campaign urging citizens to do the right thing. Police officers responded swiftly; the defective bomb made from fertilizer and gas was defused. The terrorist Shahzad was captured at the airport boarding a Royal Emirates flight out of New York.

The plot is but one of a long string of obsessive and destructive plans for mass murder in one of America's greatest cities. For terrorists, New York's attractions include great towers, Wall Street, the Statue of Liberty, busy ports and transportation hubs, and almost any mass gathering of citizens. Even the presence of the United Nations (UN) headquarters building infuriates Al Qaeda and its comrades, who declaim the organization as a tool of the United States, inherently anti-Muslim, and an enemy of their own plans for a multinational Muslim caliphate. "The blind sheik," Egypt's Omar Abdul Rahman, whose followers conducted the 1993 attack on the World Trade Center, had the UN building on his list of projected targets, along with the Holland Tunnel linking New York and New Jersey.

For two decades we have seen one attempt after another to rend New York City with a massive attack on civilians. Here are examples of what followed the first truck bomb attempt against the twin towers. In March 1994, a Lebanese named Rashid Najib Baz opened fire on a van transporting Hasidic youths over the Brooklyn Bridge; one rider died and three more were injured. In mid-1997, West Bank Palestinians Gazi Ibrahim Abu Mezer and Lafi Taisir Khalil entered the country over the Canadian border and took up an apartment in Brooklyn, where they prepared a suicide vest and nail bombs for an attack on subway riders.[3] Police raiding this safe house also found a portrait of "Sheik" Rahman of Egypt. September 11, 2001 hardly needs mention; there is an astonishing audiotape, released three months after the tragedy, of Osama bin Laden and close associates (perhaps huddled in Kandahar) exulting about how the results of the 9/11 plot exceeded all hopes, and praising Allah.[4] In 2009 came another plot against the subways, with direction from senior Al Qaeda planner Adnan G. el Shukrijumah, apparently working from Waziristan in northwest Pakistan.[5] The same year saw pre-emption of a plot by four men seeking to deploy man-portable missiles to shoot down military planes at a New York air base, and use explosives to blow up a synagogue in the Riverdale section of the Bronx.[6]

New Yorkers share such dangers with the rest of us, and Bostonians still getting over the shock of the 2013 Boston Marathon bombings are not the only concerned citizens. Consider that sprawling metro area, Washington, D.C. The Capitol, the White House, and the Pentagon are all targets of today's terrorists. One Al Qaeda journal recommended shooting up noted restaurants in D.C. when the "power lunch" crowd could be victims. A run of incidents and plots in recent years underscores how acute the threat is for *any* of our large metropolitan areas. Portland, Oregon, escaped a car bomb plot in late November 2010; the target was a gathering for a Christmas tree lighting in a public square. One year before, on Christmas Day, 2009, in a plot begun in Yemen, "Underwear Bomber" Umar Farok Abdulmutallab flew from Amsterdam toward Detroit. Intelligence later suggested that the Motor City was selected in part due to the differing prices of air tickets for various U.S. destinations—an entirely banal reason for murderers to consider. As victims, any Americans would do.

Smaller cities and towns are also potential targets, and any concentration of Americans is targetable according to the illogic of the new partisans of religious war. Even single assassinations are highly recommended. Instructions are available to any of the "self-radicalized" readers of such Al Qaeda organs as *INSPIRE* magazine, which began publication in Yemen in 2010. As he moved closer and closer to bombing Fort Hood in Texas in July 2011, suspect Jason Naser Abdo was carrying instructions for bomb-making from this journal.[7] In New England, in early 2013, one of the Boston Marathon bombers had *INSPIRE* logged into their home computer; their very attack would be lauded in the next issue, no. 11 (May 2013). For *INSPIRE* readers, "Jihad as individual duty" is a central precept of Islamist dogma, and open exhortations to "terrorism" remove any doubts about whether "jihad" is merely personal spiritual struggle. The same theme runs through the many writings of ideologist Ayman al Zawahiri, now the most authoritative of Al Qaeda leaders. Even though Al Zawahiri is a surgeon trained to heal, he can busy himself penning instructions for the common man to use in killing Americans and other infidels with such simple tools as a knife or an iron bar. This perverse counsel echoes advice in the Al Qaeda manual[8] discovered by police in Manchester, England, and used as evidence in subsequent trials of Al Qaeda men: the public could see the clinical detail in which assassinations and larger-scale attacks are planned and described, employing poisons, "cold steel," or other deadly means.

## A Changing Picture Since the Cold War

The post-Cold War age is a fortunate one in most ways. There have been no uses of nuclear weapons and no major world wars. We have not been attacked in a conventional war, and the last of those (when Russian invaded Georgia) left our immediate interests untouched. The collapse of the Soviet Union and the Warsaw Pact swept away scores of state agents busily supporting international terrorist groups. If Russia's return to despotism is serious, and even deadly (for a few Russians who have been regime critics), at least Washington has peaceable relations with Moscow. North Korea, while bizarre, embedded in international crime, fascinated by nuclear technology, and threatening war on South Korea, is not killing Americans. Although it does still skirmish with South Koreans, North Korea was removed from the official "state sponsors of terrorism list" by the George W. Bush administration. China has lost most of its Maoist fervor, and while its defense budget keeps climbing, its conquests of late are economic, not geographic. Our past enemies, Germany, Italy, and Japan, are today's best friends, models of liberal democracy and partners when we need them. The North Atlantic Treaty Organization came to our side in the 9/11 crisis, declaring that "an attack upon one is an attack upon all," and today NATO is larger and perhaps more capable than ever before.

But we find the world still troubled by several state sponsors of international terrorism. Iraq and Libya have worked themselves off the shortlist maintained by the Department of State. Still on the list, however, are the northern half of Sudan and Cuba—although neither state has been acting very aggressively on the international stage. High on the list are Syria and Iran. This pair has made an unequal but successful partnership for three decades in aiding Middle Eastern terror groups, especially Hamas, the Palestine Islamic Jihad, Hezbollah of Lebanon, and Saudi Hezbollah, all of whom have killed Americans. An Iranian armed unit, the Revolutionary Guards' Quds Force, attempted in 2011 to use an Iranian American with Mexican contacts to murder the Saudi ambassador to the U.S. while he was in Washington, D.C.[9] By 2013, Quds Force combatants were directly committed to fighting to protect a key Iranian ally, Syria's government, which was tottering. Tehran also takes care of Lebanon's fierce Hezbollah and shovels money, arms, training, and documents to sub-state actors making war upon Israel, other neighbors, and Western interests.

During recent years it has become undeniable that Pakistan is a state sponsor of terror. This sometime-partner, sometime-plague replies to international criticism by saying, first, that it is the victim of terrorism; and, second, that it has aggressively pursued Al Qaeda, killing, capturing, or extraditing many. Both points are true. But overwhelming evidence ties this restless, nuclear-capable state to a range of other bloody incidents and groups, especially the Taliban, who contest the elected government of Afghanistan. Kashmiri separatists of Lashkar-e-Tayyiba (LeT) not only enjoy Pakistani support as they carry on each year damaging democratic India; communications intercepts also show a Pakistani ISI (intelligence) officer in a command-and-control role during the horrific LeT attack on civilians all over Mumbai in November 2008.[10]

To these state sponsors of terror (Iran, Syria, Sudan, Cuba), and to Pakistan, which has not yet been formally designated,[11] we must add smaller surprises on the international stage. Power hungry and violent, sometimes as technically adept as state foes, are the militant groups that political scientists call "sub-state actors." The post-Cold War world knows more of them than it would want, and in diversity that at times bewilders. Old nationalisms still fester as on the island of Corsica where scores of minor terrorist attacks occur each year. Other militants recall with hope the brief empowerment of fascism in Europe and Asia during the 20th century: in the Czech Republic, Russia, Hungary, and the United States, these neo-Nazis work to advance their stunted dreams. Their opposites—anarchists, who condemn all government save perhaps local councils with no power—imagine themselves to be on the rise in Italy and in Greece, and the latter country is terribly vulnerable. New groups in Africa, and older ones in Latin America, prey upon the international oil companies and local businesses. The Lord's Resistance Army in Africa, a transnational troublemaker, claims adherence to the Ten Commandments but is in the businesses of child slavery and mass murder of villagers. That is akin in its way to the tragic distortions of religion and politics of such willful leaders as Ayman al Zawahiri of Al Qaeda and the Taliban's Mullah Omar. Such militant groups are dangerous to Americans today, and given their lust for weapons of mass destruction may be more dangerous than certain small foreign countries. Indeed, since 9/11, the UN Security Council's language about terrorists has often equated them to major state aggressors.[12]

Consider Aum Shinrikyo, part religious cult and part failed political party. This Japanese group made four different gas attacks in 1995,[13] including the sarin gas deployment on multiple subway cars, sickening 5,000 people in Tokyo in a few hours, and permanently wrecking the lives and health of hundreds. Its scientists also made biological weapons, while other Aum cadre were hunting uranium ore on land bought in Australia. They plotted anthrax attacks in Japan coincidentally alike to the one that actually occurred several years later in America. Probably made by one lone warped U.S. scientist, that attack killed five U.S. citizens and injured 17 more in a "terror-by-mail" campaign of late 2001. The specter of an actual plague of anthrax cannot be ignored. Our public health system is unprepared for an outbreak of smallpox or many other diseases. Right-wingers and certain other Americans, and Islamists of contemporary days, have shown fascination with the plant-based toxin ricin, famously used by the communist bloc Secret Services in 1978 to kill a political opponent. West European authorities have uncovered ricin plots in several countries, and the recipe for making the poison from beans is spelled out in the Jihad manual of Al Qaeda.[14] Islamist revolutionaries are interested in other kinds of poisons as well. France arrested Islamists in possession of a nuclear/biological/chemical warfare suit, and then, in 2004, arrested an Algerian called "The Chemist," trained in Afghanistan's camps. Chlorine gas was used in several insurgent attacks in Iraq. Italian police interrupted a 2002 plot to deploy cyanide gas in a utilities service tunnel underneath our embassy in Rome. The tape of an eerie telephone call proves how the Moroccan perpetrators hoped to deploy cyanide crystals to yield the gas that would suffocate Americans working above in the building. In one case, if not more, terrorists have plotted to undertake a strike inside the United States with a "radiological dispersal device," a limited amount of nuclear material scattered by conventional explosive. Fortunately, such nuclear material is a technical challenge to handle, however small the amount.

The danger of mass casualty attacks is not limited to specialized high-tech weapons, however. Ours is a country with semi-automatic weapons and tens of millions of other guns. The kinds of terrorist plots to unfold include those by individual shooters, as at Los Angeles International Airport (July 2002) and an Army-Navy Career Center in Little Rock, Arkansas (June 2009). Other plots have been based around a group of terrorists assaulting with simple but deadly hand-held weapons, which are easy to procure and to transport in a free society. This was planned at Fort Dix (January 2006). It was Mumbai, India, that suffered a "model" assault: in November 2008 a dozen men trained in Pakistan tore at the large, peaceable, and modern Indian city, shooting citizens as if they were penned rabbits. The terrorists of Lashkar e Taiba ("Army of the Pure") evaded authorities for more than two days, killing ceaselessly. Lesser but tactically similar attacks with small arms have occurred at others' hands in the Middle East and elsewhere. A military commander of Al Qaeda, Saif al Adel, is reported to favor the Mumbai style of attack by the Militant Islamist International. And for would-be murderers who cannot find teammates, Al Qaeda organs such as *INSPIRE* publish details on how a single militant could burn down his apartment complex, or use a welding machine to turn the pickup truck in his garage into a sort of scythed war chariot.[15] Hate-fueled imaginations do not merely run wild; their conceptions are printed in color for study and adoption by the "faithful." Many Americans recognize the danger in such tactics and wonder aloud "why it hasn't happened here?" The answer is that it can. It may. It did in central London with the audacious knife attack by two Islamist men in May 2013.

As many Americans have learned since 9/11, the self-proclaimed "jihadis" believe they are at war, call for more war, and are conducting war, on whatever scale they can manage, day by day, and worldwide. Their motives can be understood and will be addressed in the next chapter. What it means for us is serious. Here at home the threats are manifest, and Americans have seen a lengthening line of plots (blessedly interrupted!). And U.S. citizens venturing abroad, whether tourists, officials, or humanitarian aid givers, are under new dangers. Scandinavia, once seeming immune, now encounters small-scale but lethal violence tied to Middle Easterners and Islamist terrorists. June 2011 saw a new conviction of conspirators in the plots against staff of a Danish newspaper; Chicago businessman Tahawwur Rana was jailed for supporting the conspiracy. And some Scandinavians are supporting "holy war" in Syria. Democracies that are not only "liberal" but also famously gentle and indulgent—such as Holland and Spain—have seen their easy parameters tightening, their societies twisted with new tensions created by a new enemy within, whether recent immigrants or radicalized citizens.

The new dangers are well illustrated by one Israeli counterterrorism expert when he tells audiences of a pattern in his consulting work abroad. In many a city hall or national office where he has offered his consulting services, he has been told confidently: "Terrorism is a problem *you* in Israel face; we don't have it *here*." He was told this in Argentina, before Hezbollah and Iranian agents carried out two massive bombings of Israeli and Jewish targets in Buenos Aires. He was told this in Holland, before the stabbing of filmmaker Theo van Gogh, and other terrorist attacks transformed the national and social environments. He was told "not to worry" in Indonesia, but in Bali a vehicle bomb aimed at tourists and nightclubbers turned a city block into rubble and left 200 dead. He was told this in Spain before the Al Qaeda affiliate the Moroccan Islamic Combatant Group placed a half-dozen bombs aboard passenger trains converging upon Madrid, killing 200. Little wonder that such consultants—and others abroad, such as Executive Action, Blackwater (now "Academi") and G4S Wackenhut—have been so profitable in the last two decades. Companies and communities are afraid. When government does not provide security, citizens willingly overpay private firms for defense.

Two decades ago, a parallel American story took a similar path, and faced *us* with a nasty reality. Our government went through a cycle starting with the first (1993) blast at the World Trade Center and running straight through two declarations of war by Osama bin Laden and the Africa embassy bombings of 1998. One could say the parts of this cycle were: refusal to believe; recognition in some quarters; study of the Islamist threat and limited learning about it; hard work at advocacy by some parts of the government for countermeasures; escalating warnings; disaster on 9/11.

This American experience is also suggested through the story of one personality working for the Federal Bureau of Investigation, John O'Neill. After years of trying to persuade colleagues in the FBI and associates in the security business that "Al Qaeda is coming," O'Neill closed out 20 years by retiring from government service. For this expert on international terrorism, it was no trouble to find private employment—at a salary twice what the Department of Justice could muster. O'Neill signed on to be head of security for the World Trade Center, with an office on the 34th floor of the north tower, from which his domain of seven buildings spread out in view. He started work there on August 23, 2001, and openly told colleagues and friends he was placing himself in the center of the bulls-eye, that something big was coming from Al Qaeda, that they *would* try a second time to knock down the towers. On September 11, John O'Neill was on site, at work. Not killed in the first tower's collapse, he was last seen doing his job, headed into a tunnel under the second tower. His body was later found in the rubble mountains. Being prescient did not save his life, nor did dedicating his life to watching Al Qaeda.[16] He led, but even he could not bring along "the whole of government" in doing what was required for the national defense.

Being complacent will not save our lives. It is important that Osama bin Laden was killed on May 1, 2011, and that the following weeks brought the deaths of two more Al Qaeda figures: Ilyas Kashmiri (a major planner in the Waziristan gray zones of Pakistan) and Fazul Abdullah Mohammed (who orchestrated 1998's simultaneous embassy bombings in East Africa). The spring of 2012 saw the demise of Abu Yahya al-Libi (Mohammed Hassan Qaed), the latest to be Al Qaeda's senior operations officer. But principal commanders and strategists remain at large, beginning with the prestigious veteran, skilled organizer, and leading author in Al Qaeda: Dr. Zawahiri. The larger point (on which I have the agreement of Jim Phillips, one of America's most reliable analysts of the Middle East) is that this long fight has never been with one individual; Al Qaeda has always been an *organization* and the base of a larger *movement*. Our struggle is against both. The movement is enlivened by a poisonous ideology—"violent extremism," the State Department calls it—which remains global and powerful, non-dependent upon individuals such as Osama bin Laden. The movement also has a revolutionary "vanguard" of veteran leaders. Along with them are hundreds who have been through an Al Qaeda camp in the Sudan, Afghanistan, Pakistan, or in East Asia. Ayman al Zawahiri had already joined Al Qaeda, and was helping to direct those very encampments on the day of 9/11. Behind the leaders stand thousands of supporters worldwide, including the newly awakened and self-radicalized small cells and individual terrorists—perhaps the most difficult to anticipate or to stop.

We are safer, now, after this long interval than we were on 9/11. But we are not as safe as we should be.

## Notes

1  The group's full name is Tehrik-e Taliban Pakistan (TTP) and according to the Department of State its claim to have aided the Times Square bomber is valid: "TTP directed and facilitated the plot," according to *Country Reports on Terrorism: 2011* (Washington, D.C.: GPO, 2012).

2  Accounts of federal prosecutors, according to Benjamin Weiser, *New York Times*, September 30, 2010. Shahzad told a judge he had "made a pact" with the Taliban and spent 40 days with them in Waziristan, Pakistan, receiving five days of bomb training.

3  Terrorist actions involving crossings of the U.S.–Canadian border are listed in the author's *Terrorism Today*, 2nd edition (New York and London: Routledge, 2007), 28–29. An excellent if dated source on incidents in the United States is

Louis R. Mizell, Jr., *Target U.S.A.: The Inside Story of the New Terrorist War* (New York: John Wiley & Sons, 1998). More current on Canadian matters is Stewart Bell, *Cold Terror: How Canada Nurtures and Exports Terrorism around the World*, 2nd edition (Toronto: John Wiley & Sons, 2007). There was also a serious Al Qaeda plot in 2012 to 2013 to blow up a train and bridge connecting the United States and Canada.

4  The Department of Defense released the three-part tape in December 2001. One of its translators was serving at Johns Hopkins University, and a professor there, Dr. Mary Haybeck, confirms for me the authenticity of the tape.

5  Charlie Szrom and Chris Harnisch, "Al Qaeda's Operating Environments" (Washington, D.C: AEI, March 2011), 2.

6  Department of Justice, *Today's FBI: 2010–2011* (Washington, D.C.: GPO, 2011), 24.

7  News sources including the *Washington Post* of July 29, 2011.

8  Four "lessons" of this 18-lesson manual have been on the FBI's website. The English typescript of the original is 180 pages long. George Washington University scholar Jerrold Post arranged a nearly full edition, *Military Studies in the Jihad against the Tyrants: The Al Qaeda Training Manual* (Maxwell Air Force Base, AL: USAF Counterproliferation Center, August 2004).

9  See David Crist's "Epilogue" in *The Twilight War: The Secret History of America's Thirty-Year Conflict with Iran* (New York: Penguin, 2012).

10  The LeT gunmen kept in touch with ISI via cell phone while deciding where and whom to attack next during their rampage. This has been widely published and is also confirmed by a 30-year veteran officer (retired) of Indian paratroops, Berham Sahukar.

11  The behaviors of these states are described by the Department of State in *Country Reports on Terrorism*. Another source is the Hoover Institution's Thomas H. Henriksen, *America and the Rogue States* (New York: Palgrave Macmillan, 2012).

12  The UN has now declared terrorism "a threat to the peace," which had always been UN trigger language indicating state aggression.

13  Richard Danzig, Marc Sageman, et al, *Aum Shinrikyo: Insights Into How Terrorists Develop Biological and Chemical Weapons* (Washington, D.C.: Center for a New American Security, July 2011).

14  In the Jerrold Post edition of the manual cited above the ricin recipe is excised, an act of discretion.

15  Vehicles have been used in terrorism to deliberately run over victims—most recently in the London attack on a serviceman in May 2013; two assailants hit him with their car and then killed him with knives. A Nablus (West Bank) resident drove a car into a group of police outside a nightclub in Tel Aviv on August 29, 2011, jumped out, and stabbed bystanders with a knife. Years before, at a North Carolina campus, an individual male student (whose earlier terrorist plots were foiled) drove his SUV into a crowd of American students, injuring over half a dozen. All of these perpetrators made obvious their desire to make "holy war."

16  Lawrence Wright, "The Counterterrorist," *The New Yorker* (January 2002) and *The Looming Tower: Al Qaeda and the Road to 9/11* (New York: Alfred A. Knopf, 2006), ch. 19.

# 2

# THE NATURE OF THE
# ENEMY TODAY

Colin Powell, who had the misfortune to be Secretary of State on September 11, 2001, has reflected: "Every one of us was affected ... . Some of us lost loved ones ... . Others of us merely lost our innocence. We can never look at a jetliner flying in a clear blue sky the same way again."

For Steven A. Emerson, the losses on 9/11 must have cut like a razor. He had authored several books about terrorism, even before 1993, the year of the truck bomb beneath the World Trade Center in New York.[1] After that nearly catastrophic attack, Emerson turned to film to amplify his message. *Jihad in America*, his documentary, exposed on audiotape and videotape the sorts of persons who are living here in America, yet eager to rip this country to pieces. The documentary was astonishing for two reasons: first because of its foresight and, second, because of the way in which it went largely ignored by academics and media. The film opens and closes with Emerson speaking quietly into the camera, the two great towers of the World Trade Center framing the background. So passed 1993 and 1994.

New York's day of doom in September 2001 found citizens of 62 countries in the twin towers. A surprising number of Central Americans perished. One Yemeni newspaper ran a headline saying 300 Muslims died in the towers. How many representatives of the world's other religions fell—or leapt—to their deaths that day is unknown. Secretary of State Powell added that the attack killed Muslims, Jews, Christians, and Hindus. He said: "Muslim leaders around the world have condemned these attacks. Leading Islamic groups have joined distinguished Muslim scholars in rejecting bin Laden's efforts to cloak himself in Islam."[2] It is not only Americans, but the world community, who also face this enemy. Our main enemy is the Militant Islamist International—as broadly dispersed as it is narrow minded.

It is silly to suppose that this terrorist enemy is our own creation— although some here and abroad dare to say so. Overwhelmingly, Americans do not and never did abhor Muslims; Americans abhor terrorism, and we see plainly that much of terrorism today comes from self-proclaimed Muslims. Many of these attackers scream "Allahu Akbar" ("God is Greater") and similar slogans in Arabic, as in the skies above Manhattan[3] and on the ground at Fort Hood, Texas, where Major Nidal Malik Hasan wounded and killed army colleagues— until heroes without weapons subdued him. Similar kinds of spoken appeals and confessions by terrorists have been captured on tape or in transmissions of cell phones as death looms—for example, during the massacre in Mumbai, India. Confronted by so many illustrations of how the killers say what they mean, victims and other citizens would have to be blind to deny that religiously inspired ideology is at work. U.S. statesmen have been ever so careful to not call this "a religious war," but senior Al Qaeda spokesmen do so regularly. No revelation is needed; we must merely pay attention: today's Islamist terrorists are among the more forward, loud, and prolific publishers of all time.

There is another reason for dealing with this current terrorism challenge on its merits, rather than fretting that our country is gripped by anti-Muslim obsessions, as do commentators in the school of Noam Chomsky.[4] The United States came face to face with, resisted, and outlasted two other major waves of terrorism in the late 20th century. First came Marxist-Leninists of the late 1960s and 1970s; they lit up world news wires, and our embassies in Latin America, and our bases in NATO Europe for several decades. That generation of terrorists included Weathermen and black militants here at home; Latin American comrades of Che Guevara and Fidel Castro; Italy's "Front Line" and "Red Brigades" and other "reds"; Germany's Baader-Meinhofs and other leftists. Then, second, there followed something of a wholly different sort: America faced a rising of the right wing, here at home. "Militias" armed and rehearsed for a fight with the federal government. The old Ku Klux Klanners recruited and carried on. Violent, self-blessed racist "churches" included Aryan Nations, the Phineas Priesthood, and the World Church of the Creator (later renamed the Creativity Movement). Neo-Nazis such as White Aryan Resistance and The Order had their day. "Lone wolf" operators bombed gay bars or Internal Revenue Service offices, shot Jews or killed cops, or hunted abortionist doctors for political purposes. These (generally) right-wing terrorists held too loose a mix of differing political objectives to be as coherent or enduring as militant Communism, but they did their damage, peaking in the truck bombing of the federal building in Oklahoma City in 1995.[5] All of these killers and would-be killers of the American political right were listed in the annals of political crime published by the FBI[6] and lavishly covered by the media. So, older Americans of today have faced terrorism before—at least two waves of it—before the encounter with Islamists of current motivations.

U.S. citizens today are not joined in some mass, incomprehensible outburst against an unfamiliar religion. But we *are* facing a distinctive and muscular third wave in contemporary terrorism: a violent Islamist wave.

This new violence was foreign in origins but is increasingly able to infect and militarize individuals within our borders. The lethal edge of contemporary "Islamism"—an ideology more than an inner faith—may be found in writings by unusual extremist Sunnis—the Sunni faith being the main branch of Islam. These writings include *Milestones* and other work by the Egyptian Sayyid Qutb, who lived for a time in the United States of the 1950s and thought Americans to be sex crazed.[7] As well, there were influential works by Pakistan's Sayyid Abul Ala Maududi,[8] and epistles of other angry, thoughtful men. Iran's revolution of 1979 was a watershed in two ways. It was seeming proof that Islam could rule a state again, as the faith had in so many centuries past. Secondly, Iran is a powerhouse of the Shia faith, a branch normally at odds with Sunni Islam. Yet, within three years of achieving power the Iranian mullahs were backing terrorists of *both* branches of Islam. Tehran supports Hamas and Islamic Jihad, both exclusively Sunni. Tehran's favored sons, however, are the Shia of Hezbollah in Lebanon, who developed a cult around suicide bombing, a skill re-demonstrated in Burgas, Bulgaria, in the July 2012 murders of Israeli tourists.[9]

During the late 1980s in Afghanistan, the Saudi Osama bin Laden and the Palestinian Abdullah Azzam founded a services bureau to aid those in combat against the Soviet Red Army—a motive few could question given the communist occupation. But the Afghans' victory over the USSR made some participants, especially foreigners from the Middle East, hyperventilate and inflate their aspirations. If the most aggressive and militarist world power of the time—the Soviet Union—could be defeated, they imagined no one could stand up to "Holy Warriors." Al Qaeda, "the base," was created to take their fight to the whole world; its doctrine elevated above all else in life the narrow and violent notion of holy war, "jihad." That traditional idea, not often invoked in the 20th century until its last decades, was changed by hammering. Recently it has emerged as a new terrorist doctrine demanding enlistment of all Muslims in all places, making it a strict and individual duty to be ready to kill whenever opportunity arose. Declares the spring 2011 issue of *INSPIRE* magazine: "Terrorism is a religious duty, and assassination is a Prophetic tradition." The article, in part about "praiseworthy terrorism," cites what seems the single most-favored Koranic quotation for terrorist propagandists, Surah 8, al-Anfal: "And make ready against them your strength to the utmost of your power, including steeds of war, to strike terror into (the hearts of) the enemies of Allah and your enemies, and others besides ... ."[10]

Few terrorist gangs in history have kept so long an enemies list. "Apostates" who stray from the faith are leading targets. The 180-page Jihad manual of the 1990s was directed at them above all, and Al Qaeda delights at the fall of many "insufficiently Islamic" governments during the great revolutions in the Middle East and Northern Africa of spring 2011. Rival Muslims of all brands are reviled, as in Pakistan, where religious factions murder one another to a degree matched only by terrorist casualties in Afghanistan. Jews, not surprisingly, are always called a legitimate target by Islamist extremists. "Crusaders" abounded in history, which lives afresh in the minds of Islamists a millennium later. America is deemed to be on a new "crusade," despite the White House's repeated disavowal of that word.[11] America is also denounced as the "new Rome," a sprawling, secular savage empire. Americans, whether civilian or military, are explicitly targetable. All these enumerated "categories" of human beings are detestable, killable enemies. A world that has seen fascism, and genocide, now gapes at a newer form of systematic dehumanization.

Why?

Like most terrorists in history, the new breed in Al Qaeda and its international affiliates prize action more than thought, violence and clandestine organization more than prayer. But their lust for violence and action does not make them non-religious or non-political; they can be both. Their faith, ideas, and murders must be understood together. Consider the examples of two Al Qaeda partner groups, both "successes" in world terrorism: Jemaah Islamiyah of Indonesia and the Taliban of Afghanistan; neither group is Arab, of course; yet both are fervently Islamist. Continents apart, both organizations literally emerged from religious schools, led by a mix of clerics and teachers. It follows that these men—for they are nearly always males—do state goals and do consider closely the means to those goals. One must study them, as with any enemy. In foreign policy, and in war, one can often discern what other states and political entities desire and how they work toward it; we seek to identify "policy" and "strategy."

The leading policy (declared objective) of the new violent Islamists is to re-establish the caliphate. The caliphate existed in many past eras and is sought now in renewed form. It is a conception of a pure and transnational entity in which *sharia* law based on the Koran and the other revered texts is the only principle for governance. The Muslim nation is to be reborn, and an Islamicized constitution will replace most existing government of Muslim peoples. The separation between church and state in modern democracies is never to be imitated. And the international system of states is openly repudiated—especially the United States and its allies, but also the United Nations; all of these international partnerships and organizations are deemed secular and hostile to Allah's word. On many occasions since 1996, Al Qaeda spokesmen have addressed these goals. As more and more Americans take note, there has been increasing attention to Islamist activists here, as well as in Britain, Germany, and other democracies. Communities have begun countering those who want to give *sharia* a place in our common-law courtrooms. Islamists lobby to have Koran-based law affect our decisions in family law and other matters; but some U.S. states and localities have already formally voted against any such foreign influence in constitutional law or judicial procedure. Observers of these pressure tactics have called them "lawfare": strategical use of courts in an ideological struggle.

The strategies (ways toward their objectives) of the international radical movement vary. Some groups, such as the Muslim Brotherhood (including Egypt's short-term President Mohamed Morsi, 2012–2013) emphasize political action and even denounce violence. They hope to advance the future caliphate slowly and without a fierce backlash. By contrast, Islamist terrorists think that approach naïve, or at least see themselves with a different role. Like Vladimir Lenin's "revolutionary vanguard," with a network of militants worldwide, each acting in support of the same goal, Al Qaeda's core and its affiliates are hoisting flags, inspiring followers, and organizing their warriors and terrorists, their lobbyists and lawyers. Our newspapers run recurring articles that say Al Qaeda is now "decentralized," which is true. But in many respects *the organization was founded to be so*; it is comfortable fighting in varied and non-hierarchical ways. Al Qaeda at this stage seeks allies and influence over public opinion, more than direct control of populations, as would traditional insurgents. They use "the propaganda of the deed," as did 19th-century anarchists, to seize attention, damage their enemies' prestige, and undermine the power of existing political regimes.

Al Qaeda is not as strong or as deep today as it was in 2000. But Al Qaeda thinks, and it thinks in *grand strategy* terms, with awareness of multiple forms of power. That is clear from the "trifecta" of their targets: the World Trade Center, the Pentagon, and the U.S. Capitol (which they missed when the plane fell short in Pennsylvania) tell us volumes about the varieties of economic, military, and political damage they strive for. All are useful to their purposes. Scores of videotapes, yet more audiotapes, and declarations and interviews have poured forth to argue their case, explain their targeting, and appeal to the world. These sources document the multifaceted way in which Islamist terrorists understand power. They value many forms of power, and many kinds of struggle, in pursuit of announced ends, which are religious, political, and fanatical.

Success need not come *soon*. There are few to no indicators of impatience, and no hard schedules, in the strategic documents of Al Qaeda Central.[12] Osama bin Laden had his reasons for saying so often that he was in this fight "until Judgment Day comes." It did, for him; for hundreds of his cohorts and trainees, that fate still awaits. To a U.S. citizen, as for an analyst of strategy, this holds out horrid prospects of endless low-intensity conflict. Even Leon Trotsky, the Bolshevik favoring "permanent revolution," expected to achieve communism one day *on earth*. Al Qaeda's important ally the Taliban, now largely focused on events within Afghanistan and Pakistan, is just as patient: insurgents have quipped to our Coalition soldiers in Afghanistan: "You have the watches, but we have the time." Taliban fought from 1994 through 2001 to come to rule 90 percent of Afghanistan, but lost their political power to our invading coalition. Since about 2004 they have grimly fought back, and again rule large swaths of the territory. The world is watching "Taliban the Second Time Around."[13]

Among the parallel Al Qaeda strategies that show us the organization of this enemy is economic war. Is it naïve to think that an economy as large and resilient as ours could be broken by an international terror organization? Surely. Yet, Al Qaeda speaks openly of its "bleed until bankruptcy plan." Their strategy against the U.S. economy is one of attrition, death from a thousand bites. 9/11 cost us as much as U.S.$100 billion, a figure bin Laden inflated (in a speech later) to U.S.$1 trillion in losses of all kinds. But all can agree that this was just the beginning. Al Qaeda continues hitting economic targets. Oil is one priority, although since the French vessel *Limburg* was damaged in 2002, most further plots have failed; the Saudis have blocked many stabs at their fuel depots and refineries.

From Yemen, the "how to" journal *INSPIRE* has advocated slowly strangling the West in economic knots. When two bombs built into computer printer cartridges on UPS cargo airplanes failed to cause explosions, the magazine pushed out a special edition in November 2010. It proclaimed that "Operation Hemorrhage" was a success: even if no planes were downed, it provoked us into a massive and long-term security effort that was enormously expensive. And that is true. Near misses also inspire general fear, true terror, which is even more rewarding to Al Qaeda than the losses in dollars poured into security instead of the directly productive investments we would all prefer for our economy. It is fully consistent with this strategy for Al Qaeda to boast about the low price tag on the multiple "pressure cooker bombs" that tore limbs from Bostonians on an April day in Massachusetts in 2013.

In military terms, Al Qaeda sees itself as practicing guerrilla war. This form of war is as old as man[14] and there is nothing inherently illegal or immoral about it if modern "humanitarian law" is observed during its conduct. Guerrilla war is the use of special tactics and units to surprise and attack military targets. Like most past and present terrorist groups, Al Qaeda strikes at armies or their supporting structure *on occasion.* This is dangerous for the attackers and far harder than terrorizing "soft"[15] civilian targets who cannot fight back—the latter being Al Qaeda's specialty. And these pin-pricks against military establishments are never decisive. But Al Qaeda can always get volunteers: not all of them insist upon surviving the mission; some burn with desire to "go straight to heaven" and enjoy imagined rewards. Above all, these limited assaults on martial targets are symbolically important. Each advertises courage and suggests the semblance of a true army. Attacks on our military also indicate an elevated view, something above the level of a mere gang that hacks off the heads of reporters, aid workers, and other civilians. While decapitations provoke terror, military strikes imply professionalism. The determined attack that cracked open the *USS Cole* when it came to Yemen in a port call is a worthy example of the enemy's military side. It took 12 years to find and kill the planner, the man named as Fahd Mohammed Ahmed al Quso of Yemen, gone at last from the FBI's "most wanted" list.

The political nature of the terrorist enemy also drives it toward diplomacy. As unlikely as it seems, diplomacy *is* sometimes practiced by terrorists. In most foreign capitals, the Algerian Front for National Liberation of the late 1950s outmaneuvered the French. The Palestine Liberation Organization warmed up friends via Yasser Arafat's address in the United Nations General Assembly in 1974—an honor not given to even the presidents of many countries.[16] The Tamil Tigers of Sri Lanka and the Irish Republican Army have shown competencies in such open politics. Al Qaeda, for its part, has no formal diplomatic corps; lacking legitimacy and credentialed by no state, their envoys would be arrested upon appearing publicly in almost every foreign capital. But the group has its own strategy as one of the cyber-originators of *public* diplomacy by sub-state groups—the modern art of going around a foreign government and directly to its people.

The dimensions of Al Qaeda's own public diplomacy include use of the Internet and such interested news stations as Al Jazeera TV to make broadcasts of its sophisticated and well-produced videotapes. There are, as well, the foreign language publications, including arguments and inducements in idiomatic American English penned by American members of Al Qaeda; two such Americans died in a U.S. drone strike of October 2011. Perhaps for the first time in our history, an American president, of the Democratic Party, has apparently sought and achieved the killing of an American citizen hiding abroad, Anwar al-Awlaki, a traitor famous for enemy propaganda. The cleric was known to directly inspire attacks, including the shooting massacre committed by one Muslim American doctor at Fort Hood in Texas. It is not surprising that such action by the White House has excited public debate; during the 20th century, even the assassination of *foreign* terrorists living *abroad* was deemed illegal and bad form. Discussing the option in public was "just not done" by American politicians or generals.[17]

Consistent with their targeting and with their many public declarations, Al Qaeda proceeds by interlinked, parallel approaches along lines that are political and economic, as well as military. Their grand strategy emphasizes violence: economic damage; foul terrorism; and clever guerrilla warfare. Their publicity campaigns shout out for open, indiscriminate violence but are just as capable of fine poster art, appeal to sentiment, and sophisticated argument. Terrorism is the lead weapon of the Islamist movement; this is classic "propaganda of the deed." But following closely is more formal propaganda: the audio cassette; the DVD; the web essay; the targeted interview. High education and intelligence levels in the Al Qaeda leadership ensure future use of strong and, at times, original methods.[18] While they cannot win their war with us, and with the world, their war surely continues, uninterrupted by the death of bin Laden.

## Notes

1  Emerson's early books include *The Fall of Pan Am 103* (with Brian Duffy) and *Terrorist: The Inside Story of the Highest-Ranking Iraqi Terrorist Ever to Defect to the West*, about Adnan Awad of the Abu Ibrahim Group (written with Christina del Sesto).
2  Colin L. Powell, "United States' Position on Terrorists," November 19, 2001, reproduced in the periodical *Vital Speeches* (December 15, 2001), 131. My address at the Department of State on "Advancing U.S. National Interests: Effective Counterterrorism" appears in the same *Vital Speeches*.
3  "The Last Night," a document of guidance prepared for "the day of the planes" (9/11) hijackers includes the advice: "When the confrontation begins, strike like champions who do not want to go back to this world. Shout 'Allahu Akbar,' because this strikes fear ... ." Next is a passage about the beautiful women said to await them in paradise. The letter was released by the FBI and translated for the *New York Times* by Capital Communications Group and published on September 29, 2001.

4 This linguist at the Massachusetts Institute of Technology (MIT) steadily issues books on terrorism, mostly hyper-critical of American policy. They are popular in Europe: I have seen multiple different volumes in a Rome store; in London one shelf offered 11 titles; I saw 17 Chomsky titles, all different, at another London bookshop. Issue 11 of *INSPIRE* quotes his criticism of "American terrorism."

5 A useful text on the complexity of competing ideas in rightist extremism is Daniel Levitas, *The Terrorist Next Door* (New York: Thomas Dunne Books, 2002).

6 Regrettably, the Bureau's "Counterterrorism Threat Assessment and Warning Unit" of the Counterterrorism Division ceased publishing the *Terrorism in the United States* series after 2001—at the very time more Americans would have wished to read it. Instead, the FBI offers different, less regular reports on terrorism, or directs readers to other U.S. agencies' products—but those usually lack focus on incidents in America.

7 An Egyptian born in 1906, Sayyid Qutb (Mohammad Qutb) was executed by his government for sedition and terrorism. A member of the Muslim Brotherhood, he became famous promoting Islamist ideology and contempt for the West.

8 Born in 1903, Maududi edited a journal, founded the Islamic Party, and worked in Pakistan until his death in 1979, writing much about the ideal Islamic state.

9 Much was learned about this Hezbollah attack from Cypriot court proceedings against a man who confessed; *New York Times*, March 22, 2013.

10 Abu Mus ab Al-Suri, "The Jihad Experiences: Individual Terrorism Jihad and the Global Islamic Resistance Units," *INSPIRE*, no. 5 (March 2011), 29–32. For the full Koranic passage 8:60, Dr. Douglas Streusand of the U.S. Marine Corps' Command and Staff College provides me with the N. J. Dawood translation: "Let not the unbelievers think that they will ever get away. They have not the power to do so. Muster against them all the men and cavalry at your command, so that you may strike terror into the enemy of God and your enemy, and others beside them who are unknown to you but known to God."

11 Perhaps thinking of how Americans such as Dwight Eisenhower spoke and wrote of World War II as a "crusade" (e.g., *Crusade in Europe*), President George W. Bush once called the war with Al Qaeda a crusade. Uproar ensued. White House retractions over subsequent years did not quell all critics, foreign or American.

12 One of the few to seem intent upon firm plans, al-Suri, has written reservedly about "phases" of the struggle. But in the new Arabic language edition of *Knights under the Prophet's Banner* (2011) Ayman al Zawahiri writes (according to Dr. Norman Cigar of Marine Corps University) that al-Suri is not officially a member of Al Qaeda.

13 A gifted graduate student, Jessica Groves of Missouri State University has completed an (unpublished) Master's thesis on the creeping return to power of the Taliban—for which I suggested the title, employed in the text here.

14 Robert Asprey chronicled 2,000 years of guerrilla war history in *War in the Shadows*, first released in two volumes in 1975. The newest book of similar

theme, by another fine historian, is Max Boot, *Invisible Armies* (New York: Liveright/W. W. Norton, 2013).

15  Issue 11 of *INSPIRE* magazine by Al Qaeda exhorts readers to bomb crowds and other "soft" targets.

16  On PLO diplomacy, see Paul T. Chamberlin, *The Global Offensive: The United States, the Palestine Liberation Organization, and the Making of the Post-Cold War Order* (Oxford: Oxford University Press, 2012).

17  As a lecturer on counterterrorism I saw this public reluctance and spoke of it. It was quite revolutionary when Ronald Reagan's defense secretary Caspar Weinberger asked publicly, in the journal *Strategic Review*: "Can We Target the Leaders?" (Spring, 2001), 21–24.

18  Many of the Islamist terror group leaders, and sometimes cadre as well, have high education levels, especially in technical matters that help in their plots. The pattern is visible in the September 2011 news that a 26-year-old physics graduate from Massachusetts conspired to use drone aircraft to carry bombs into the U.S. Capitol and the Pentagon.

# 3

# BARRIERS TO OUR OWN DEFENSE

As the first two chapters indicated, the realities of terrorism are ugly and common, as common as the daily newspapers. So, what kinds of barriers have prevented us from being properly defended? There are numerous obstacles, which come in many types and vary in their legitimacy. We begin with the least worthy justification for inaction.

One explanation of why some people decline to act against terrorism lies in the psychology of appeasement. We recall how in the 1930s Italian and German fascist parties held sway over their own countries while intimidating others into inaction. Peoples who were still free spoke of their fear of a Second World War, and diplomats hunted for new ways to appeal to mutual interests in order to moderate the hostile and land-hungry capitals of Rome and Berlin. So strong was the urge to avoid the fascists' geopolitical challenges that our "pacifists" became "militant" in their manners, feeling obliged to shout down the rare statesman who accurately described fascism's ideology and expansionism. Thus, Winston Churchill was hooted at when speaking to students at Oxford University for discussing the war plans of enemies then in action. Some students and other citizens just preferred not to know—probably because it would require responsible action ... by someone.[1] The appeasers were terribly wrong. Unchecked, aggression did not wither, but grew.

Today's new totalitarians differ. They are not states but "sub-state actors" bent on forging a new transnational and Islamic super-state ("the caliphate"). So they repudiate traditional nationalism. The new totalitarians are also ideologues, violent to the core, and as bent on war as any 1930s fascist. They do not just hate the system, they mock and attack the moderates who would reform the system, seeing them as counter-revolutionary. They aspire to lead a global movement, not just a narrow organization. Once in power they would govern as totalitarians. The Taliban—glutted with success in capturing most of Afghanistan in the late 1990s—whipped women for letting an ankle be seen beneath a coat, and threw acid into the faces of girls so bold as to go out of doors unveiled. In October 2012, irritated with a 14-year-old girl who was publicizing her education, they hunted and shot her. The Taliban has blown up religious statues and burned down scores of public schools—whether built by the Afghan government or international aid agencies. Yet some still imagine that such gunmen may be appeased or "brought into the political process." Such a policy is deeply impractical, and when so many crimes are being committed, it may be immoral too. The Taliban are terrorists—not just insurgents and religious fanatics. They cannot be appeased and they do not want "a part" of the political process; they are bent upon rule.

A second layer of resistance to opposing the Militant Islamist International movement is the conviction—or argument from misunderstanding—that before fighting terrorism, we must *first* "deal with the roots of terrorism." This is often a petition to escape from acting, observes Andrew N. Pratt, a Germany-based director of a global counterterrorism program. Certainly, terrorism has "roots"; it is not done in a fit of passion. In the cases of famous Palestinian terrorists as different as Leila Khaled and Abu Nidal, the two charged the new state of Israel with taking over their family lands. There might be other connections between Palestinian terrorism and refugee camps, and we should not deny that poverty and hopelessness can be a recruiter to militancy. But one form of deprivation or abuse does not justify another that deliberately assaults the innocent or the later generations. Secondly, how could poverty explain—in developed countries such as Uruguay and Germany and Spain—*their* experiences of widespread terrorism in recent times? Meanwhile, many desperately poor areas such as the slum belts around Latin American cities are *not* producing international political terrorist groups. Any causal link between "economic deprivation" and terrorism is unproven and tenuous. The United Nations lacked a basis for its statement, in 2002, that terrorism results from "oppression," which in turn is usually "economic oppression."[2]

Where does discussion of this second barrier leave the American citizen as to national policy? Not demanding a revolution, or the eradication of Israel. Responsible Americans, and their government using general tax revenues, have for decades supported anti-poverty programs run by the UN and others in Palestinian refugee camps, and fostered education via lasting institutions. The United States might well do more—and it is, by supporting the new Palestine Authority in the West Bank. It is reasonable for U.S. citizens to favor such political and humanitarian aid efforts while *also* opposing the homicidal bombers who sally forth from Palestinian camps. Both responses are appropriate. If we are really to deal with the roots of terrorism, it is vital to see that it is about power and political ideas more than poverty.

A third kind of barrier to opposing this modern political violence is definitional. In legal and academic circles, one often hears that "there is no approved international definition of terrorism." Of course, the same is true of "war," or "property rights," or "love"; yet nobody denies that those are real. Terrorism is as real, even if every thinking adult can see how the term could be misapplied. Admittedly, U.S. agencies and U.S. codes have kept a variety of definitions. And in the post-9/11 period when the United Nations and the world community are increasingly accepting of the principle that terrorism is an evil form of political action, Barack Obama's State Department has chosen to avoid (on most occasions) the term "terrorism." This White House has a preference for a broader, more nebulous phrase: "violent extremism."

But the Departments of Justice, State, and Defense largely agree. None uses a definition of "terrorism" that would bar a legitimate revolution against despotism, or block a state's appropriate use of special military forces in war. U.S. departments hold that *terrorism is directed against innocent non-combatants, for political purposes*; that it is usually done by political or ideological minorities *using shock tactics to attract national and international attention*; and that terrorists thus *seek to intimidate wide audiences and win political change*. In the various definitions of terrorism around the world, those characteristics usually appear. In 2002, the United Nations adopted a very workable definition in its convention for the suppression of terrorist financing. Finally, the "political offense" exception which used to open many anti-terrorism accords to abuse has all but disappeared. Interpol has abandoned its notion of a "political exception" and now tracks terrorists as carefully as it does the criminals who are only after money. There is a growing international understanding that a terrorist is a terrorist is a terrorist ... in any country.[3] States should keep moving in the same direction, and so should our academics who, as a group, have been more quarrelsome than helpful in the matter of adequate definitions. Terrorism is *violence directed more against the audience than the target, designed to promote a political cause.* The goal might be forcing a government to change its policies, inspiring fear in an enemy and destroying their society, pleasing the divine, or punishing moral transgressors. Each of these goals applies to Islamist terrorism, but all terrorism seeks some political end of this nature. Terrorism is violence for the cameras, meant to alter the world to fit an ideological image.

Limitations on manpower have been a fourth barrier to our proper defense. An office can only develop so many intelligence leads, given the numbers and skills of its employees. Work against terrorism often competes with good work against other forms of evil or crime or need. The Federal Bureau of Investigation was watching terrorism, and prosecuting terrorists, before 9/11. But its main focus was internal to the United States and many of the "watchers" were at work against white collar crime, congressional corruption, child pornography, gangs, and a dozen other legitimate concerns. Only eight weeks before 9/11, Attorney General John Ashcroft rebutted staff who wished to raise terrorism on the FBI's priority list; he seemed to think it had climbed enough already. Ashcroft barked at a senior aide: "I don't want to hear about that anymore ... . I don't want you to ever talk to me about al Qaeda."[4] Even if he had placed terrorism first, his focus might have been on the individuals and tiny groups who target federal buildings, "lone wolf" terrorists creating poisons, cells seeking shoulder-fired missiles, or eco-terrorists burning down meat packing plants in the hope of elevating "animal rights." The Bureau had more work to do than most agencies *before* 9/11; *since* then its agents have worked hours as long as those of our military forces deployed in hostile zones. There are not enough hours in a day. This may help to explain why a "lead" on one Boston immigrant from the southern Russian periphery might go unnoticed by the FBI in 2012, before the Boston Marathon bombing.

Another barrier to our proper defense, number five, was built by misguided officials and bureaucratic allies and is called "the wall." This is shorthand for a complex of administrative regulations and policies built around a suspect idea—firmly separating American authorities' work on international terrorism and foreign intelligence questions, on the one hand, from U.S.-centered domestic functions of criminal indictment and prosecution, on the other. Created in reaction to excesses of spying and covert action during the 1970s, "the wall" or "the Chinese Wall" was protected and added to by earnest people determined that our foreign intelligence agencies, such as the Central Intelligence Agency, must never peer into the privacies of Americans at home. That it did. An FBI man trying to track a foreign terrorist suspect within the United States might actually be unable to open a file, or clip a news report about the man being stopped for a traffic offense, or check telephone books to see where he lives without risking disciplinary action. The CIA, reportedly, could stonewall the FBI over what foreign intelligence there was on those who attacked our warship *USS Cole* in Yemen—even though the FBI sent scores of agents there to investigate and prepare for a possible trial. The FBI, for its part, was at times criticized for withholding what it knew from everyone, U.S. or foreign. "The wall" blocked analysts of terrorism cases from seeing all that our analysts of criminals did, and vice versa. Since most terrorism breaks domestic and criminal laws routinely, this was a terrible blunder.

"The wall" was maintained and enlarged in the 1990s. One of the busy masons was Clinton Defense Department Counsel turned Deputy Attorney General, Jamie Gorelick. Another bricklayer, working right up into September 2001, was a Justice Department specialist on the Foreign Intelligence Surveillance Act, Allan Kornblum.[5] After 9/11, American citizens were astounded to think that known Al Qaeda men had boarded commercial aircraft in Boston and other airports. How could government fail to "connect the dots?" The melancholy truth is that one reason we could not see Al Qaeda coming was that we had blocked off our own view, brick by unnecessary brick. The exchange of intelligence is much better now, but it can be inhibited by the culture and protocols of our different agencies and to keep it flowing requires the continuous efforts of senior supervisors.

Other challenges—a sixth type—face our government when it attempts to deal with terrorist groups abroad. American foreign policy must have priorities among the many competing considerations. Washington wrestles with scores of foreign policy issues each day. Even those leaders who care deeply about fighting terrorism know there are other important issues. Two decades ago a young army major, wise beyond his years, told the author that "The problem with our counterterrorism is that it has to compete with all the other U.S. foreign policy interests."[6] No one could better or more briefly state this common barrier to counterterrorism. Part II of this volume will illustrate this challenge.

Overseas, and seventh among the barriers to our proper defense, is foreign indifference—which is also a leading problem for Americans at work building conventional military alliances that include the United States. Despite the clear duty under international law—both traditional and modern—some foreign states utterly fail to oppose terrorists. At times their neglected mess ends up in the American backyard. Worse, a few foreign states propagate and export terrorism. Countering terrorism thus requires ongoing efforts and strategies to work with foreign partners and to take international roles that we may or may not want. When a foreign state has not been slammed with terrorist violence in the way the United States has, its government finds it easy to ignore how its territory is being used to train or provide refuge to fugitives from justice. A state such as Cuba knows where every violent foreigner is within its borders and may let them stay—defeating any Interpol notices or U.S. requests for extradition. And a Cuban neighbor such as Honduras or Mexico, *not* being totalitarian, may be host to a violent foreigner or domestic terrorist without knowing or likely caring. Limited or defective government is common worldwide, increasing the challenges of combating an international movement. A score of Latin, African, or Asian countries do not even count the dots, let alone connect them. Usually this is not a civil liberties issue as in the United States or Europe; instead, it is inability. The United States has new programs with some such states, but they must come far before they can secure their own borders. So, when intelligence identifies a new trafficking route moving Latin American cocaine eastward across Africa and up into Europe with the involvement of terrorists, it does us little good unless the governments of the Saharan belt can help us make use of the new intelligence. U.S. military advisors and counterterrorism experts worked steadily with Mali throughout the last decade, improving many aspects of that African country's internal security. But that did not mean Mali could resist invasion by well-armed guerrillas of the Al Qaeda type in 2012; France (helped by American airlift) had to rush in troops to liberate Timbuktu and other towns. To offer a last example, when some in Pakistan want to fight Al Qaeda, as they do, the indifference or outright collusion of many other officials in that country can undermine everything, which it does.[7]

Apart from indifference, there may be principled refusal to help Washington, an eighth barrier to our proper defenses against terrorists. Some good ideas and offers meet with flat refusals. We have close partners in Europe who disdain certain U.S. requests for extradition over the capital punishment issue; they will pointedly refuse to send us a fugitive—however air-tight the legal case against him—if he might be given the death penalty. In other cases it is a refusal based in muddle—not morality. In October 1985, after the ship-jacking of the *Achille Lauro*, Egypt allowed the hijackers to fly away to freedom aboard a commercial aircraft. U.S. combat jets forced their plane to the ground in Sigonella, Sicily, so that the terrorists might be captured. But Italy disliked the appropriation of its air base in that way, quite apart from its generally good relations with America. Italy's specialized police units and U.S. commandos on the ground had a stand-off, guns pointed.[8] Years later, during the global war on terrorism, it appears that Italian intelligence did the opposite—directly helping with the rendition of a terror suspect off the streets in Milan so that he could be interrogated. Yet this led to trials within Italy for the officials, and impositions of some severe punishments. These very different cases may point some Italians in one direction, in the future: defend sovereignty rigorously and be wary of an ally's requests. In such cases two warm friends and NATO allies can part ways temporarily.

Ninth, in opposing terrorism, we deal often with blunt foreign multinational opposition. Washington has rivals and, on occasion, enemies who combine in the United Nations Security Council. The council's rotating membership brings aboard such states as Syria and Venezuela, and other rivals or enemies are often in place as votes arise. These groups oppose U.S. initiatives; in fact, China or Russia can veto many U.S. proposals even without partners in the voting. Iran nearly always opposes U.S. interests and ideas in UN forums and can form small alliances. Long the leading state sponsor of terrorism, Iran has recently harbored famed terrorists such as Imad Mughniyah of Hezbollah (d. 2008), certain leaders of Al Qaeda, including military expert Saif al Adel (who now may have left Iran), at least one of bin Laden's sons, and an Al Qaeda finances man, Yasin al-Suri, an ethnic Kurd and Syrian citizen. Yet the country invariably escaped sanction by the United Nations! This began with the Ayatollah Khomeini regime in 1979. With 52 Americans held hostage[9] in our embassy in Tehran during the Carter administration, Washington introduced a censure motion into the Security Council. But the Soviet Union, an exporter of terrorism and a UN Security Council permanent member, vetoed it. Never since has Tehran paid any appropriate price for its enthusiastic and overt support to Islamist terror groups. President Obama has pushed for multilateral sanctions against Tehran.

Governments such as Iran's deserve a robust response by the United Nations. It is not only capitals such as Washington, Tokyo, and Berlin that have duties to deal with terrorism, but also Ban Ki-moon and the UN headquarters. This must begin by checking states such as Iran that introduce terrorism into international relations and then blocking legitimate counterterrorist efforts.[10]

Thus far we have considered the breadth of the terrorists' challenge, as well as the impacts upon Americans and our interests, and nine of the barriers that inhibit our proper defense. We now turn to what makes for effective counterterrorism, and examine how our national strategy is working.

### Notes

1  This insight about inaction in international affairs is owed to the teaching of Harold W. Rood (d. 2011).

2  *Global Terrorism*, an academic study guide by the UN's Institute for Training and Research, for its Program of Correspondence Instruction, dated 2002; see 372–373.

3  "One country's terrorist is another country's terrorist" was the rejoinder to relativists by Dr. Paul Wilkinson, a founder of the related graduate school at St. Andrews University called the Centre for the Study of Terrorism and Political Violence.

4  Garrett M. Graff, *The Threat Matrix: The FBI at War in the Age of Terror* (Boston, MA: Little Brown and Co., 2011), 173, 280. Fran Townsend is another official who reportedly helped to build the wall during the Clinton years; she then headed George W. Bush's Homeland Security Council.

5  *The 9-11 Commission Report* by Congress (Washington, D.C.: GPO, 2004), 269–271; 424. See also, op. cit., Graff, *Threat Matrix*; consult the index under "Chinese Wall."

6  U.S. Army Major R. Rachmeller, then a student at the Naval War College, in a discussion with the author; Newport, Rhode Island, 1991. Such officers taught me much, and their successors do now.

7  Lashkar e Taiba, Harakat ul Mujahedeen, Hizbul Mujahedeen, and other groups fighting for Kashmiri independence, and fighting against Americans in Afghanistan, are trained, funded, and armed by Pakistan, especially through its intelligence service ISI, according to reports—for example, *New York Times,* July 4, 2011.

8  Italians on the Naval Air Station grounds were Carabinieri and a unit called VAM. The stand-off with U.S. forces lasted long minutes. Four gunmen from the Abu Abbas group "Palestine Liberation Front" were taken off to Italian trials and jail. But they served minimal time for the ship-jacking and murder of Leon Klinghoffer. One by one they were later allowed to slip out of Italy. The end for the small PLO sub-group came when the United States and allies invaded Iraq in the spring of 2003: Abu Abbas was captured and later he died.

9  Six Americans (including an associate of the author) escaped with the help of Canadians, but 52 others within the embassy building suffered 444 days of captivity.

10 Our enemies' attacks are not aimed only at Americans. Indeed, their promiscuous targeting should assist in forming multinational coalitions against terrorism. Islamist terrorists and revolutionaries say that they are assaulting the system of states and the norms of international relations. The UN is to Islamists a terrible enemy—for its principles, its constructs, and its troop deployments in blue helmets. Thus the New York City United Nations headquarters was targeted by self-proclaimed "jihadists" in 1993. In August 2003, the UN building in Iraq was blown to bits, killing two dozen aid officials and diplomats. After that bombing, the claim from the Abu Hafs al Masri Brigades, an Al Qaeda organization in Iraq, "explained": "The United Nations is against Islam ... . [It is] deaf, dumb, and blind, and void of wisdom," and "infidel." The press release also described the international body as a mere tool of American policy and raved: "We will overcome the United States and cut its despicable veins; I, Oh Bush, am a terrorist with nails and fangs of iron." The procession of assaults on United Nations offices continued. April 2001 saw terrorists attack an aid office in the Afghan town of Mazar Sharif and murder three UN employees. In August 2011 came a bombing of a UN headquarters in Abuja, Nigeria, that killed two dozen people and wounded four score; the murdering group, "Boko Haram," means "Western education is forbidden." June 2013 saw an attack on the UN in Somalia, more of this global campaign by Islamists.

# Part II

# THE STRATEGY

# 4

# COMPONENTS OF OUR
# GRAND STRATEGY

## Diplomacy, Intelligence, Economics, Law, and Law-making, the Military

The American people and government hold many advantages in this fight with the international Islamist organization called Al Qaeda, and our advantages will ultimately mean victory over such terrorists. The United States can draw upon immense economic, military, and political powers: allies—some of whom recognize the mutual threat from Al Qaeda and its affiliates; intelligence-gathering capabilities the world has never seen in its history; and the dedication of innumerable government and military personnel, whose sheer numbers outrun the operational rosters of Al Qaeda Central today.

However, for these advantages to affect the battlefields and back alleys of anti-terrorist operations, they must be well orchestrated. And synchronizing competing bureaucracies, as well as disparate overseas partners, is exceedingly difficult. The president and his National Security Council (NSC, or National Security Staff), as well as relevant congressional committees such as foreign relations, armed services, and intelligence, have a challenge that no government can envy. Defeating Al Qaeda, its allies, and the broader violent Islamist movement is a challenge these busy public servants have begun—but not completed. Our future depends on a favorable outcome. So this chapter examines the most important tools of American power, with an eye to assessing how well the strategy may be working.

Grand strategy is the art and process by which all the tools of a nation's power are brought to bear—in this case, against global terrorism and its archetype today, Al Qaeda. Grand strategy applies to "the home front" as well as to our foreign affairs; it once seemed that most attacks came against us overseas, but 9/11 has made it obvious that both domains must be watched. Grand strategy must be made in peacetime as well as war; when terrorists attack, they plunge us into just that "gray area" between war and peace. The more we wrangle and wrestle among ourselves over whether our fight is military or just "law enforcement," whether terrorists are "guerrillas" with prisoner of war (POW) rights or just violent criminals, the more the terrorists thrive in their war in the shadows. One adds to this the complications of law and law enforcement by American officials and service personnel in sovereign countries such as Iraq and Afghanistan, where the complications are many, and political, and sometimes lead to the release of insurgents or terrorists after capture.

How does our government attempt to sort all this out and give direction?

The process begins with periodically publishing documents on counterterrorist strategy. The most important of these are not the "top secret" memos that are leaked occasionally to favored newspaper writers. The most significant documents are public, available at www.WhiteHouse.gov and other Internet sites. These begin with the *National Security Strategy*, which Barack Obama published in May 2010. This document lays out the president's priorities for the nation. Such national strategies express the character of a given administration, following in a long line of similar documents from past White Houses.

Second in importance, subordinate to the larger strategy paper, is the *National Strategy for Counterterrorism*, released in June 2011. It follows, but differs from, others published by George W. Bush in 2003 and 2006. The differences begin with the title: President Bush called his a *National Strategy for Combating Terrorism* (my emphasis added). Another difference in the two administrations is reflected in a supplementary, shorter publication that this White House has issued on *Empowering Local Partners to Prevent Violent Extremism in the United States* (August 2011). This reflects an initiative by the Obama administration[1] in an area in which past presidents have not often worked, though others such as the Netherlands and the United Kingdom have been active in this area for many years. The drive to stop "violent extremists" at local levels is reasonable, a response to horrors the Dutch government saw in the street-knifing of a film director in November 2004, and what the British government saw in a similar street knifing of a serviceman in May 2013.

Important U.S. agencies have their own documents which should, in theory, reflect the White House priorities. These include a marvelous resource by the State Department called *Country Reports on Terrorism*, which appears annually and covers events and programs of the last year (see www.state.gov). There are also unclassified documents of great value from the Department of Defense, such as a *National Military Strategy of the United States* (last released by the Pentagon in August 2011) and a more focused Joint Publication 3-26, *Counterterrorism* (November 2009).

U.S. military strategies *vis-à-vis* counterterrorism have changed less than most citizens realize. Certainly the Obama administration's withdrawal from foreign wars in Iraq and Afghanistan has received much attention; but his new engagements in Libya and Syria somewhat offset the image of a pacific Democratic Party. In counterterrorism, more strictly understood, the White House is carrying on with many of the objectives Mr. Bush sketched during the early war against Al Qaeda and its affiliates. The first George W. Bush strategy of 2003 announced four pillars of national strategy, and they remain a valuable conceptual architecture—even now with reduced federal budgets:

1 Defeat terrorists and their organizations.
2 Deny them sponsorship and sanctuary.
3 Diminish the underlying conditions that terrorists exploit.
4 Defend U.S. citizens at home and abroad.[2]

More than a decade after this long war began, we as a nation retain our central goals. These begin with defeating and destroying the architects of 9/11, Al Qaeda Central, and its affiliates. We must separate those littler craft from their mother warship: the enemy is a network, so our international coalition is working to divide and contain Al Qaeda's affiliates and support structures worldwide. This is the "disarticulation strategy" enunciated by an Australian turned U.S. senior advisor, Dr. David Kilcullen. Second, we are also (if less successfully) contesting the ideological substance and prestige of the Militant Islamist International. Our national strategy recognizes that Al Qaeda is more than an organization; it is the vanguard of a movement, a leader in an ongoing war of ideas. Those poisonous ideas incite action and so they, too, must be contested and their conceptual and spiritual ideas exposed.

Meanwhile, our offensive and defensive efforts against state sponsors of terrorists must carry on in accord with our established national principle of opposing all terrorism as illegitimate. Students of international relations understand that, as of the late 1960s, terrorism is a primary tool of policy for some. Violent communist insurgencies still infest Colombia; the PKK Kurdistan Workers' Party still kills in Turkey, and anarchists are a new threat to parts of Europe. Terrorism will never be eliminated, any more than all crime can be stopped in Detroit or Los Angeles. But as terrorism is, by definition, an attack on a whole polity, it must be brought down to the lowest manageable levels, to a point at which it no longer poisons our daily lives with fear. War is rarely required in counterterrorism, but continuous effort—sometimes including uses of force by police, the military, or an ally—is required.

Multifaceted efforts, coordinated with domestic U.S. and foreign partners, is the rule for good grand strategy for countering terrorism. By design, that places our National Security Council squarely in charge. Working intimately with the executive branch, NSC staff should be at the center of decision-making in a "whole of government" approach.

To a degree, the current documents (introduced just above) inform us about many of the things government is actually *doing*. The following chapters attempt to show more—for there is much more—while also demonstrating the challenges of connecting these various strands of strategy, and connecting our ends with our means.

## Diplomacy

Turning from documents to practices, American tools of strategy begin with diplomacy. It is legitimate to wonder why diplomacy counts, given that terrorists lack the legitimacy of national governments, that they transgress state borders illegally for violent purposes, and that many terror groups do not even aspire to become a state. On the other hand, the United States is constituted as a sovereign state and always proceeds as such; this is also true of most of our foreign partners in the counterterrorism fight. These sovereign partners have an embassy in our capital and vice-versa; they may have consulates in our larger cities to facilitate business, immigration, and other issues, including counterterrorism. National political entities offer well-established means of communication. And they often share our interests—such as enhancing trade, advancing peace, and working together to contain a regional aggressor. Quietly, our 7,000 diplomats and other embassy employees work each day, usually in ways helpful to our counterterrorism missions. They do not always get full respect for their work: an old joke has it that "An ambassador is an honest man sent to lie abroad for the good of his country." Nonetheless, diplomats are highly useful instruments for international work against the transnational plague that is terrorism.

It is true that feigned agreement, loose promises, and half-truths are parts of international politics, and all of these do turn up in anti-terrorist "diplomacy." An example is the strong posture that governments such as ours take against negotiating with terrorists; academics enjoy pointing out examples of where, in fact, even the United States has done so.[3] Distortions of this nature will also occur in multilateral efforts in which numbers of capitals and interest groups jostle for what they want. But in action against an international terror group, a larger number of "players" can lend international legitimacy to the public side of the game and enhance its practical results. Few Americans think of Ethiopia as a security partner, but in fact that country has done superb work against Al Shabab ("The Youth"), Somalis now integrated into Al Qaeda terrorism. And most Americans would doubt that the soldiers of the African Union would be as capable as, say, the French Army or the U.S. Marine Corps in a task such as blocking "Janjaweed" Arab militias from marauding through Christian and black African communities in the southern Sudan. But for that particular combination of terrorism and ethnic cleansing conducted by Janjaweed, the African Union holds more natural legitimacy as an opposing force. African Union capitals throughout the continent can and should bear responsibility for the Sudanese crisis and its resolution, now complicated by the recent division of North and South Sudan. Practically speaking, U.S. armed forces have too many other duties in many other places more related to U.S. vital interests—especially when the White House wants our forces to "pivot" toward Asia in line with the newest thinking on U.S. strategy reflecting the rise of China and challenges from North Korea. It is thus a "plus" for global security and counterterrorism when the African Union intervenes in the Sudan. One may welcome its collective decision, and its 10,000 uniformed police and troops.

Two clear cases of multilateral success in recent years deserve mention in our considerations of how diplomacy may increase our power and legitimacy against terrorism. The Irish peace process of 1997 to 2007 has rightly captured imaginations—it seems to have dramatically reduced violence and pointed a clear way ahead. An old IRA chieftain, Martin McGuinness, has appeared as Deputy First Minister of Northern Ireland shaking hands with the Queen of England. The Stormont Parliament building outside Belfast is reopened and resounds again with the bustle of staff and the crackle and sting of debate between many parties as it governs the northern counties that traditionalists call Ulster. The Irish and English stock of Northern Ireland are governing their affairs together again. The participation by fractious and sometimes suspicious Irishmen of either "loyalist" or "republican" bent is key to the future. Their affairs had been governed directly from London/Westminster during the generation-long crisis that began in about 1970. Diplomacy's long campaign to bring accord has largely succeeded. The drive was led by competing Irish politicians and aided by skilled officials in London. U.S. mediators of great help included Democratic Senator (retired) George Mitchell, whose great skills commended (and condemned) him to a follow-on assignment in the turmoil of the Middle East. President Bill Clinton took the Irish peace cause under his wing, making our good offices available via his National Security Council staff. The remaining violence has been limited to some fresh youth and a scattering of old terrorist hands who either have no other employment or harbor hatreds too deep to soothe. Violence—usually non-lethal—has continued from 2008 through the present, tracked by terrorism experts such as John Horgan. The Irish and the British can stand it, and so can we. Diplomacy brought the parties together and brought forward solutions, creating a far sunnier future for Ireland than seemed likely in 1970 or 1980.

A second success involves Libya. While the results have been confused by later controversies in Libya, the lessons of this example from 2003–2004 are clear about diplomacy's possibilities. Diplomatic processes led to Libyan renunciation of its elaborate efforts to gain weapons of mass destruction (WMD). These programs had reportedly advanced in all categories: chemical, biological, and nuclear. In the hands of a Colonel Moammar Qaddafi, no regional neighbor (and no citizen of America) could feel assured catastrophe would not come. But instead of invasion, the West led with negotiation as the strategy for de-weaponizing Libya. It worked. British and American envoys from the diplomatic and intelligence worlds labored together and *did* bend Libyan policy.

The U.S. negotiation team was led by Steven Kappes (the number 2 man at the CIA) and diplomatic counterpart Ambassador Robert G. Joseph, who published a revealing memoir about the efforts.[4] Inducements to the Libyan government doubtless included prospects of selling oil and the end of decades of sanctions. There were also, to be sure, subtle threats. There was the surprising arrival of Coalition troops in Iraq not far away in March 2003; later Qaddafi admitted how this seized his attention. What is clear is that Qaddafi repudiated his weapons programs and allowed sweeping international inspections of suspect sites. After 2004 there is also little to no evidence that his regime exported terrorism. This from the government that all but invented the practice of terrorism export in modern times, supporting every group imaginable: Irish "Provos," Abu Sayyaf allies of Al Qaeda, Palestinians of the Abu Nidal Organization, even a few right-wingers in Italy during the early 1980s.

Such bilateral relations as the U.S. and U.K. partners used in the case of Libya offer a sort of intimacy in politics which can enhance the likelihood that ambassadors or lesser officials may reach accord on some mutual problem. During the 1980s, British Prime Minister Margaret Thatcher labored personally to alter the U.S. position on Irish militant refugees hiding within America. She asked President Ronald Reagan to banish the notion that a "political exception" should protect IRA suspects from normal extradition arrangements. Reagan agreed, improving the U.S. position for future mutual efforts, as when the U.K. allowed its airstrips at Lakenheath to be used by U.S. bombers striking Libyan terrorist sites in 1986. Such events furthered "the special relationship" between the British and the Americans that has so long allowed cooperation in intelligence, diplomacy, and NATO military action—to include cooperating in the 2003–2004 effort to get Qaddafi to renounce WMD.

The Obama administration—a foreign counterterrorism expert tells the author—values bilateral diplomacy to unusual degrees. He sees American work going through bilateral channels more than the multilateral sorts (e.g., the European Union; the United Nations). The president's 2011 documents can be quoted to support this analysis. In Southeast Asia, for example, President Obama's *National Strategy for Counterterrorism* boasts of "a robust network of bilateral CT [counter-terrorism] relationships with key countries ... including Indonesia, the Philippines, Singapore, Thailand, and Australia."[5] One could make a similar list for other regions.

Whether combining many partners or just two, diplomacy has an important and mixed record in counterterrorism performance. At times it succeeds; at times it merely bares the need for *other* tools of foreign policy. Cases where diplomacy helped to stop terrorism or dealt success-fully with ongoing "low-intensity war" include the little-remembered Contadora Group of nations, which had demonstrable good effects in terminating Central American civil wars late in the 1980s.[6] Finnish mediators helped to end the Aceh separatist crisis in Indonesia in 2005; diplomatic parties included GAM (Free Aceh Movement), a terrorist organization. In the Philippines, extended and painstaking efforts in the southern region of Mindanao, chiefly Muslim in character, may have worked. There was a major accord with the Moro National Libera-tion Front, which held up through 2012 but was challenged the next year. Despite one setback in mid-2011, peace processes have also seen the rival Moro Islamic Liberation Front (MILF) sign an accord with Manila.[7] MILF's ongoing work with the capital authorities includes a 35th round of talks completed on neutral ground in Malaysia (per announcement of January 2013) and labors by an international contact group including Saudis, Japanese, Turks, and British. With both groups of Moros, semi-autonomy has been the aim. If permanent, these accords will help to heal differences between the southern Muslim populations and their largely Roman Catholic counterparts to the north.

But there are many cases where diplomacy has failed. The current enthusiasm among social scientists for diplomatic prospects for "talk-ing to terrorists" invariably ignores its many failures. The Middle East's Palestinian crisis has become the career graveyard of many a skilled diplomat and well-considered blueprint.[8] Despite intensive and pro-tracted efforts with Sri Lankan terror groups from 2000 to 2006, Nor-wegian mediators failed. Tens of thousands of Sri Lankans of all sorts had perished at the hands of this "Tamil Tiger" (LTTE) insurgency, whose leadership had over three decades of experience in the arts of terror, war, and domestic and international diplomacy. When the Norwegians could not deliver the demanded concessions, the Liberation Tigers of Tamil Eelam fought on. It took a bloody conventional war involving artillery, five army divisions, other military task forces, and police to break the secessionists.

Diplomacy's most traditional role has been to foster cooperation among national governments in facing a terrorist organization. But in recent years there have been more and more cases of diplomats and special envoys working directly with terrorists themselves, which is both audacious and dangerous. If a terror group is driving toward taking state power, it will want to parlay, but not to compromise, and not to lay down arms. Diplomats dealing with such challengers may find that talks were a ploy for legitimacy. Thus Vietnamese Communists deployed guerrilla war and terrorism, and also outfoxed the sagacious Henry Kissinger and his diplomatic team in the Paris talks of the early 1970s. There is also little reason to trust terrorist envoys—unlike state servants of even the most cynical sort, they have no population or territory to protect, and there is little to guarantee their word.

One of the dangers neglected in new literature on "Talking to Terrorists"[9] is that of false negotiators. In October 2010, citizens familiar with U.S. goals in Afghanistan—to defeat the Taliban and support democratic government—may have been surprised to see parlay beginning. This might have worked were the Taliban beaten, but the gambit came when the Taliban was gaining power. Amidst naïve hopes for a favorable deal, it emerged that a primary negotiator in these quiet talks aided by NATO and Washington was a fraud! The poseur did not represent Taliban. The scandal made page 1 of the *New York Times,* a public relations disaster and a strategic failure. And then in the fall of 2011, Taliban lured a top Afghan negotiator, former President Burhanuddin Rabbani, to his death at their malevolent hands. Little wonder that enthusiasm for "talking to Taliban" waned in Washington. Yet, in June 2013, the appetite for talks somehow returned.

Past examples in counterterrorism confirm such dangers. In 1985, Palestine Liberation Front chief Abu Abbas fooled many by alleging he opposed the killing of Leon Klinghoffer on the cruise ship *Achille Lauro,* and he appeared on the stage to "mediate" during the crisis. Of course, the four gunmen in the operation were responsible to *him*, making Abu Abbas the enemy, not a good negotiator. But no one laughed. During the same year, in another hijacking, Shia gunmen murdered U.S. Navy diver Robert Stethem, and roundly abused the other airline passengers. But when the plane was on the ground in Beirut, where Shia activist Nabih Berri was Justice Minister of the national government, arrangements were made by which the killers let aboard Hezbollah guerrillas, possibly including the infamous Imad Mughniyah himself. This enlarged team, and actions it took to disperse hostages, made a clean U.S. rescue operation impossible, so none was staged, and no one has paid for the murder and the other crimes. Nabih Berri got good press as an "intermediary," which was scandalous.

One of Moammar Qaddafi's last diplomatic handouts to terrorists was equally clever. In 2000, during a hostage crisis he had helped to create in Asia by past support to Filipino Muslim terrorists, Qaddafi "intervened" to "mediate." He grandly positioned himself between his terrorist friends and the victim government of the Republic of the Philippines. A sum perhaps as large as U.S.$20 million was paid by Libya to the terrorists, according to a Filipino official detailed to negotiate. Several governments got their citizens back; Abu Sayyaf was able to buy further weapons and gear for future hostage-taking. Had the same Libyan dictator sent the same check to fund international terror *before* the crisis, such payment to Abu Sayyaf would have caused scandal. But by waiting until the right time, and casting himself as a diplomat, Qaddafi emerged as hero to all.[10]

These accounts of what diplomacy can and cannot achieve in counterterrorism close with a recent and positive example, though one largely unnoticed on the U.S. side of the Atlantic: the cooperation of France and Spain against ETA Basque terrorism. France's President Nicholas Sarkozy met with Spain's Prime Minister Jose Luis R. Zapatero in early 2008 in the Élysée Palace in Paris, presumably after weeks of elaborate work by diplomats whose deserving names do not make the newspapers. The executives cooperated against a half-century old threat, which France had been slow to recognize as a mutual enemy even though Basque terrorism affects both countries. Now many of the most important arrests come on the *French* side of the border, denying ETA its favorite refuge. While some might think a half-century old group would be ineradicable, this one is in death throes now. Much of the two governments' success resulted from their top-level diplomatic efforts, which led to cooperative policing, including one mixed unit of French and Spanish personnel. In September 2011, hundreds of ETA prisoners in Spain's jails released a shocking letter calling for the termination of armed ETA operations. That October brought an ETA announcement of cessation of armed activity (though not full disarmament or demobilization). ETA as a terrorist organization seems doomed, and a prime reason is the intimate diplomatic work between Madrid and Paris.[11]

## Intelligence

"Spying" is merely one part of the complex and vital business called intelligence. Intelligence officers teamed up with the diplomats who argued Libya out of WMD projects and terrorist operations abroad. It is intelligence officers, not only policemen, who often devote their days to hunting for terrorists—while diplomats usually deal with country officials and other counterparts. After bin Laden's death, newspapers reported on certain enigmatic agents who worked for years to locate the Al Qaeda principal, finally "connecting the dots" on the terrorist's location in Abbottabad. Few U.S. public servants—whether members of Congress or federal judges, admirals or ambassadors—are more important than first-rate intelligence officers. There is a predictable call for "more intelligence" in "blue ribbon" committee reports of the last decades penned by earnest people engaged in counterterrorist work: we depend upon intelligence and we need more of it. The cry for "more intel" is a cliché because it is so true.

Counterterrorism has a voracious appetite for collecting raw information, synthesis (putting it together), and analysis (making sense of its meaning). All of that is required before one has useable "intelligence." Where it goes wrong, or is rushed or inadequate, the operation may fail and leave a bad and lingering result. Recall how the Clinton administration, confronted with simultaneous bombings by Al Qaeda at two of our East Africa embassies in 1998, sent missiles into a Sudanese pharmaceutical plant that some thought was tied to Al Qaeda. Soil samples pointing to chemical weapons had supposedly justified this U.S. strike. Afterwards, no expert appeared publicly to affirm that the target was, in fact, producing WMD. Months of doubts dragged along into years. The United States later failed to contest the federal suit brought by the indignant owner of the wrecked factory in Khartoum.

By contrast, it was good work by multiple agencies that located, caught, and readied the legal case against the mysterious Pakistani shooter of CIA employees outside their offices in Langley, Virginia, in 1993. Mir Aimal Kasi took only moments to hit five people, but it required four years to find him. He was located by a reward-seeking Afghan informant who appeared at our embassy with a telling picture. Taliban governed most of Afghanistan then, and it protected and encouraged Osama bin Laden's men, allies, and affiliated terrorists. So an intelligence operation was devised to seduce Mir Aimal Kasi across the Afghan border into Pakistan. There he was grabbed in his sleep in a rustic hotel by Pakistani intelligence (ISI) acting with a U.S. inter-agency team. The FBI agent present[12] could verify the terrorist's finger-prints and identify him. Kasi, not wanted for crime in Pakistan, was spirited out of that country. This was a successful "rendition"—now a much derided term—and its healthy result was to put Kasi on trial in Virginia, where the crime had occurred and, as prosecutors know, a state where juries disapprove of those who murder for political purposes. Capital punishment followed in 2002. The results suited this case of a lone operator who struck inside the United States during peacetime. The intelligence process worked well; there was no clash with Pakistani authorities; the "intel" case evolved naturally into a legal case which was properly resolved.

America fights to keep ahead of Al Qaeda, other violent Islamists, and the mix of terrorist groups of very different ideological bents. As work continues, it is useful to be reminded how skill, budget, skilled people, and the sufficient attention of government are required to prevail in the fight. Not only did the U.S. agencies not "connect the dots" before 9/11, but some American leaders never understood the problem even in hindsight. In February 2005, Baltimore's Democratic mayor thought it appropriate to appear at the National Press Club and slam the (Republican) White House by comparing its proposals for cutting community development budgets to Al Qaeda "attacking America's cities." This, after Al Qaeda had actually done so.[13] The mayor's unusual comment was partisan, begging for public attention. By contrast, much of the intelligence war and the counterterrorism war, in general, are conducted in secrecy by quiet professionals who require infrastructure, equipment, training, and salaries to do their specialized work. Without full public support, they will not do it, or they may do it badly. When the mayor made his remark, a dozen other U.S. mayors of cities that—like Baltimore—had not suffered a terrorist attack should have spoken out in ringing terms for the ongoing national effort against Al Qaeda. Years on, Baltimore may still have problems, but it has not lost 3,000 citizens, or seen multiple city blocks burnt, or been poisoned by the kind of "radiological dispersal device" Ayman al Zawahiri, Jose Padilla, and other Al Qaeda men have reportedly sought to acquire without success due to international efforts to stop the proliferation of nuclear material and the U.S.-led war on Al Qaeda. Baltimore's life is not just "the status quo"; it is a success. Poverty programs, however admirable, do not deter international terrorists. Government's quiet successes are "the dogs that do not bark in the night" and they too deserve a mayor's attentions, from time to time. All politics are *not* local. Our current national budget crunch must not be allowed to wreck the security of the home in which we have lived and prospered through defeating a slew of Al Qaeda plots against the American home soil.

Much has been done in recent years to enhance the performance of law enforcement, border patrol, the military services, and various national intelligence programs. "Fusion cells" of different protective and policing services are working together, often under FBI leadership, to assess and stay ahead of local problems. These are a good idea for overcoming inter-agency difficulties and exchanging information about terrorist suspects—even if a fall 2012 government report deprecated the cells' performance to date. The Drug Enforcement Agency is expanding and has greatly improved its ability to "peer over the horizon" and check some criminality abroad, including crime related to terrorism.

The Central Intelligence Agency's budget has grown—although to what levels only specified congressional committees and the executive know exactly. And the CIA's personnel turned forcefully to countering terrorism; this commenced late in the 1990s when George Tenet was in charge and Michael Scheuer helped to shape an intelligence cell called "Alec Station" to focus on Al Qaeda. At the time, Osama bin Laden was known as a financier, trainer, and publicist of terrorism. The CIA several times located him physically—although few were willing to "pull the trigger." The CIA not only watches myriad terrorists; it helps to run the drones program that has been killing them in the field—unusual work that requires intimate collaboration with a very different U.S. agency, the Department of Defense.

Changes came to the intelligence community after 9/11. Agencies large and small are now reorganized beneath a new Office of the Director of National Intelligence, led by James Clapper. Co-located with those offices in northern Virginia is the National Counterterrorism Center (NCTC), now led by Matthew G. Olsen, a veteran of the National Security Agency and the Department of Justice. The NCTC has the mission of planning and coordinating U.S. intelligence work against terrorists. The pre-existing U.S. military intelligence organizations, and nearly a dozen other agencies, are all parts of this new centralized effort to understand terrorist networks and pinpoint their personnel.

Droves of contract workers have joined the expanded federal effort to understand the actions of, monitor movements by, translate the words of, and pursue the shipments and personnel of terrorist gangs operating abroad against Americans. A July 2010 series in the *Washington Post* seems to have exposed many of the departments of such work, or suggested locales for their reported work spaces, while estimating the number of contractors in intelligence, counterterrorism and homeland security at over a quarter-million. In part because the Obama administration has been loath to speak of a "global war on terrorism," the high numbers of contractors and their costs surprised some citizens. But while the salaries of those deployed abroad are very high, these women and men are filling gaps we taxpayers earlier refused to fund. They are doing work most Americans would not or cannot do. The salaries are also returns on past investments; legions of them had retired in past lives from the State Department or the military or intelligence organizations and have returned to redeploy their foreign languages, analytical skills, or covert action abilities. In a war, why would they *not* wish to do so? The dollar price of their services must be weighed against the larger costs of career personnel in all aspects of intelligence—the price for which the *Washington Post* did not estimate. Second, these contractor costs must be weighed against cheaper efforts before 9/11 that left the defensive gaps we now all claim to recognize. A prudent citizen would rather spend for such intelligence than see a public market in Seattle blown up, or an airport waiting zone in Pennsylvania devastated by a truck bomb. Those costs are large too—perhaps unforgivably large.

## Economics

Sanctions were an issue that roiled American politics in the months leading toward the Second Gulf War in 2003. Secretary of State Colin Powell, a man of gleaming military credentials, wanted to forgo use-of-force options and let sanctions (political and economic) have more time to work. As a statesman he knew that if sanctions do work they require a long time and full participation by the international community; a few holdouts can make a great deal of money by capturing the lucrative trade that high-minded countries are withholding. In the end, others in the George W. Bush administration fatigued by United Nations inaction and Saddam's contempt for sanctions, coaxed Powell into briefing the UN General Assembly on the U.S. movement toward belligerency.

On the level of counterterrorism rather than war, the same arguments have been common in recent decades. However well or poorly economic sanctions may work, they *are* usually a card that gets played. The most common pattern of late has been for the United States or another power to lead in sanctioning a terrorist-indulgent state, to later be joined by a slower-moving United Nations. But while it rarely leads, at least the UN may sometimes follow in the right direction, adding its international credibility to efforts by the more proactive and willing.

British and American governments long sanctioned the Libyan state for its outrages, especially the 1988 mass murder of passengers flying over Lockerbie Scotland on Pan Am Flight 103. The UN Security Council finally passed resolutions against Qaddafi demanding reasonable satisfaction for past crimes and expulsion of resident terrorists such as the Palestinian "rejectionist" of all peace concepts Abu Nidal (d. 2002). Over time, these efforts and other political pressures had effect on the regime, and Colonel Qaddafi began a limited reform of behavior. By 2005 and 2006, the United Nations and associated states were removing the strictures they had belatedly emplaced.

The story of Sudan is another revealing limited but good effect of sanctions. After the Umar al Bashir regime came to power in 1989, indulgence of Islamist propagandists and terrorism became marked.

The trend was visible in the political rise of Hassan al Turabi, a cleric who became Speaker of the parliament, and a man whose British education and personal abilities made him popular while putting opponents back on their heels.[14] Osama bin Laden was among his many foreign guests; the Al Qaeda founder lived and worked in Khartoum for five years, engaged in civil engineering projects for the regime, as well as quieter work for international "jihad." One could well argue that the international terror camps should have been physically eradicated—especially after Sudanese agents played a role in the attempted assassination of the president of Egypt. But instead the UN Security Council imposed sanctions. When they did so, in 1996, the effects were quick: bin Laden was soon moved out, or chose to move out. But Sudan's reforms were never thorough enough to make Washington remove the country from its short list of "state sponsors of terrorism." Government-sponsored militias continued to conduct especially ugly campaigns against Sudanese countrymen, mostly Christians in southern Sudan. So while Libya "earned parole" in its way, the Sudan never has. In fact, Washington favored the recent plebiscite which divided the country north from south, further isolating the Khartoum regime.

Next came Afghanistan, in part because that is where Osama bin Laden and his hundreds reappeared after leaving Sudan in 1996. They integrated into the army and security forces of the Taliban, which was capturing most of the country's provinces. American senators were among those who rightly criticized the Taliban for its ferocious mistreatment of females, prisoners, and other Afghani subjects of these enthusiasts for the rule of the black turban. President William J. Clinton imposed economic sanctions in July 1999, affecting how Al Qaeda and the Taliban could travel, stage diplomats abroad, and finance government activities. These U.S. efforts quickly yielded similar UN sanctions, which remain in place and have been reinforced by later Security Council resolutions and the "1267 Committee" administering the sanctions regime. All that took place in calm and workman-like environments before 9/11; the September 2001 tragedy moved the next U.S. president into a war mode.

In 2002 the UN implemented a major legal achievement against terrorists as individual global actors: the Convention for the Suppression of the Financing of Terrorism, now subscribed to by most of the world's 192 capitals. It offers a working definition of a terrorist act, and it demands that all signatories exert maximum effort to cut off funds and other material aid to the terrorists committing such acts. This change is significant because even when countries shamelessly ignore the treaty, our diplomats, news commentators, military liaisons, and others can strongly remind them of its explicit responsibilities. State sovereignty comes with duties—not just rights.

Use of financial tools in counterterrorism has become common, and they make an important addition to the "toolbox" available to prosecutors and to diplomats. Individuals who once blandly (or blindly) wrote checks to support hostile foreign organizations must now think twice about their actions lest they become illegal "material support" to terrorism. Citizens who work in financial institutions such as banks and import–export companies have their opportunities, and responsibilities, to watch for suspicious transactions and report them to proper authorities; such reports are required by banks, which have their own reporting duties. U.S. government specialists, as in the Office of Foreign Assets Control at the Department of the Treasury, help to track terrorist organizations which operate internationally and require transnational financial flexibility. The Secret Service works to protect the integrity of our currency against such terrorism-infected political entities as the North Korean[15] government and Hezbollah in Lebanon; both have been tied to the circulation of counterfeit U.S. bills.

We also work abroad with our major partners in the G-20, which has a Financial Action Task Force system busy since 1989 against money laundering and terrorist financing. The brilliant investigative magistrate from France, Jean-Louis Bruguière, whose career was filled with counterterrorism highlights, served until recently as our liaison to the European community for just these sorts of specialized efforts by our commercial and democratic allies.

That sanctions take time to work, and should be done multilaterally to be effective, is further evidenced by the fall of the apartheid regime of South Africa. Sanctions worked against the terrorism-exporter and WMD producer Libya. Barack Obama imposed U.S. sanctions on the Revolutionary Guards, the elite Iranian force long known for foreign operations and the training of terrorists and guerrillas; now it falls to our foreign partners to support the president's gambit; too many foreign countries prefer to have Iran's investments, oil, and other business. But in order to work, sanctions must operate internationally. Iran is the single greatest exporter of terrorism; only Syria and Pakistan are rivals. The world community can do more to press Tehran to stop.

## Law and Law-making

A short and good definition of democracy is *self-rule under law*. It follows—and the point is made in Barack Obama's *National Strategy for Counterterrorism*—that counterterrorism professionals and citizens alike must be concerned with the law as we move against our mutual enemy.

Not everything requires an explicit basis in congressionally considered, black-letter law. Frequently, governments act through administrative regulations, or managers' decisions may suffice. But practice cannot break the law and must generally accord with law. Much of the fight with terrorists is about legitimacy. They do not have it, and they seek it through a combination of politics and violence. By contrast, governments usually have legitimacy, and must labor to retain it during the struggle with the unlawful. It is not easy, nor is it easy to make good laws.

Even within U.S. agencies, definitions of terrorism vary. Military services have one; the Federal Bureau of Investigation has another. Congress also made an excellent version for the State Department, encasing it within Title 22 of U.S. Code: terrorism is "premeditated, politically-motivated violence perpetrated against noncombatant targets by sub national groups or clandestine agents."[16] These official definitions are adequate, and their differences, while questionable, are not crippling.

Democracies often struggle with the principles their laws express, protecting freedoms while meeting public needs against crime, terrorism, and extremist politics. European states work to keep their anti-terrorism laws on track, but the results include considerable differences across the continent. And even when a European capital is quite content with its laws against terrorism, an overseeing body of the European Union (EU) and its human rights courts might get involved, and that capital may be ordered to revise its legislation. For example, the European Union is critical of France, although French domestic law, policy, and vigilance blocked every attempt at a major attack in the country for a decade and a half, from 1996 until a "lone wolf" Islamist shot many, including kids, at a Jewish school in Toulouse in March 2012. French voters are used to a level of safety many states do not expect. And yet their EU comrades are demanding to know whether French voters are sufficient free, whether French Muslims' rights are protected, and the like. Usually European governments do give in to EU pressures—to keep the peace, and to stay on track with their counterparts, who all depend upon one another now that national borders have largely disappeared under the EU/Maastricht Accords.

Around the world, democratic peoples differ on how long a suspected terrorist prisoner can be held for detention before formal charges. In the United States, more than one day's interval raises red flags, and there have been court decisions saying even less than 24 hours is too long. Circumstances matter and the suspicion of terrorism may buy police greater discretion. In Greece, a suspect can only be held several days before formal charges are filed. The European Court ruled in 1980 that four days was too long to hold a suspect without formal charges. Yet the law in Britain, a birthplace of civil rights, now allows 14 days, and for years was twice that long. Indeed, the center/left Labour Party government of Prime Minister Tony Blair tried unsuccessfully for 42 days, arguing that it takes longer to decrypt the computer files and electronic messaging so common among Islamist terrorists. Only as an adjunct to battle, as in Afghanistan and Iraq, may a democratic state lawfully retain prisoners for months at a time. According to international law of war, states may do that indefinitely, until cessation of hostilities, so long as they give prisoners administrative hearings at intervals.

Another contentious issue for democracies is the proscription or banning of dangerous groups. Democratic countries—no matter how liberal or conservative—nearly all proscribe different extremist political parties. It irritates the new Central Asian democracies that Hizb ut Tahrir (HuT)—which they have banned—can have open offices in London and hear British officials defend this because of HuT declarations of non-violence.[17] Some countries ban the Muslim Brotherhood; others do not. Ironically, this movement was long banned in Egypt, the very country of its founding in 1928; but with the Arab Spring, the party briefly realized dreams. Austria prides itself on its liberality, but no one can found a neo-fascist party within its borders, even if its members never commit a violent act. Such violent extremists on the right are proscribed from politically organizing. German and Austrian history speak against such parties, and their laws against extremist groups are drafted by elected representatives, passed by democratic legislatures, and are regularly enforced by democratic-minded policemen.

Anti-conspiracy laws are as controversial as proscription and detention. There is no shortage of defenders of our civil liberties who argue that until a suspect is committing or has committed a criminal act, government can have no quarrel with him; "the state must not criminalize thoughts and conversations." However, common sense about protecting society before the axe falls, and experience with hardened criminal mentalities, has made law-makers prefer to stop some terrorist conspiracies *before* the serious crime takes place. The majority believe there are cases in which the state must act to protect rather than be caught on the sidelines watching butchery.

U.S. law (but not laws in all foreign states) protects our polity against terrorist conspiracies. The USA PATRIOT Act strengthened penalties for it, and this post-9/11 legal package is periodically renewed by votes in Congress, saving it from ending under "sunset" provisions that were built in. The principle involved is that planning and preparing to act viciously, not just the eventual lethal act, is punishable. Criminal conspiracy of non-terrorist sorts is also punishable, and few complain except Mafiosi facing racketeering charges. Even without a successful robbery, a gang can be "busted" for acquiring equipment, drawing up a plan, recruiting inside sources, or renting a vehicle as preparation. It is yet more important to protect the polity against a terrorist conspiracy. Unlike the actions of a few law-breakers, terrorist conspiracies are aimed at the general public. They seek influence and power; they may aim to shake the foundations of government in preparation for its downfall.

An anarchist's bomb, wheeled in a horse cart down Wall Street on September 16, 1920, was not only for shattering glass and the stone façades of banks, though it did so. It was almost certainly a symbolic attack on capitalism, a strike against everyone's financial security, as well as physical safety in an open society. Now a very different breed of terrorist—members of what may be called a Militant Islamist International—explicitly threaten and target British and American centers of capitalism via bomb plots. This was called for by bin Laden and some other Sunni Islamist leaders. Followers have received the message. The plot shaped by seven Americans in Liberty City, Miami, in 2006 was not just to burn down an immense building, the Sears Tower in Chicago. It was to metaphorically "raise the flag" of Al Qaeda over America in general; the perpetrators had taken the "bayat" or oath of loyalty to Osama bin Laden.

That 1920 attack succeeded—the horse cart was the first "vehicle-borne improvised explosive device" in American "terrorism," a bloody affair resulting, in part, from insufficient law enforcement against violent anarchists. Other plots for mass destruction have been pre-empted by aggressive law enforcement, who could *only* act because of surveillance, wire-tapping, and laws against "conspiracy." Some critics of arrests in the Miami case of 2006 say "free speech and association" rights had been compromised, and, after all, there was no bombing. A few other critics called these Miami plotters amateurish. More thoughtful citizens were relieved at the pre-emption. After all, it was other "amateurs" who in 1993 mixed their own bomb, placed it in a Ryder rental truck, and almost knocked down one of the World Trade Center towers. Even this "failure" injured 1,000 people, killed six, and left massive property damage. A sad ceremony in New York City in February 2013 marked the 20-year anniversary. In a world of *plastique* bombs, Internet recipes for biological weapons, and semi-automatic weapons selling for a few hundred dollars, to dismiss a plotter as a "Miami amateur" would be an offence against public safety. Given pledges to make "war" on behalf of bin Laden, their plot cannot be dismissed. For just such occasions did the USA PATRIOT Act increase penalties for terrorist conspiracy.[18]

Pre-emption of attacks, rather than cleaning up the mess afterwards, has been the new and effective policy of the Department of Justice since 9/11. Congress and courts have enhanced our ability to catch and try terrorists with the USA PATRIOT Act but also earlier decisions as to law; a few of these are detailed here for their importance.

President Ronald Reagan signed a "long arm statute" that was a signal flare about U.S. willingness to track down and grab terrorists abroad. The precedent-setting operation came in September 1987 with the luring of a Jordanian hijacker, Fawaz Younis, onto a yacht in international waters of the Mediterranean. Instead of a party with drugs and girls, the terrorist was shackled by U.S. authorities and flown non-stop westward over the Atlantic, toward imprisonment and trial. Under something called the Ker–Frisbie doctrine, related to two older cases, U.S. judges have usually been willing to hear a case, if there were American victims, discounting *where* the defendant was arrested. The new law, and the Younis case in a federal court, confirmed the principle of extraterritorial jurisdiction: "you can run, but you cannot hide."[19]

Renditions such as that of Younis may be a useful tool. Their prospects are clouded now by several years of accusations about secret prisons and torture. Cases involving good allies, Italy and Germany, have been embarrassments.[20] But the principle of rendition is sound and well worth defending. In some renditions, foreign government personnel actively help to make the suspect available to the United States—while avoiding publicity. This may occur because the individual is loathsome; but the host has less evidence of crimes by him than the American government has. Or, when the crime committed was in the U.S., it still may be that immigration laws of the unwilling "host" have been broken—a reason they would expel him to U.S. custody.[21] Rendition may well be the right and intelligent thing to do in those few cases when the evidence file is thick but normal judicial proceedings are impractical, or there is no extradition treaty, or the "host" state will not cooperate, or the exigencies of war prevail: in a few such cases, rendition may be the best of difficult alternatives.

Many citizens had never heard of "rendition" before 9/11 and now think it is a partisan issue connected to George W. Bush and Vice President Richard Cheney. It is actually an old practice in U.S. history. And in the second presidential term of Democrat William J. Clinton, the government collected three of the murderers who bombed our East African embassies in 1998, and two of those were by rendition: M. Rashed Daoud al-Owhali was brought out of Kenya, and Khalfan Khamis Mohammed was snatched out of South Africa. Clinton's Department of Justice proudly published these and other cases of rendition in normal report channels.[22] Many drug traffickers, too, have been rendered out of Latin American countries by Democratic and Republican administrations. While normal "extradition" is preferred, there are cases where this is impracticable, or where the host country prefers that the fugitive be taken away for U.S. trial quietly without press attention and political damage. At times another government actually helps to arrange a rendition; certain Sudanese probably helped to snatch "Carlos the Jackal" from Khartoum and handed him to French authorities bent on trying him in Paris for longstanding murder charges. Impressions of Carlos have been prettied up by the actor chosen for a 2010 French commercial mini-series,[23] but the actual man, murderer Ilich Ramirez Sanchez, is only in jail because a French rendition ended decades of his mocking the international community's pursuits. Renditions may even be considered small examples of grand strategy, in that each reveals the linkages between intelligence-gathering, covert action, use of force to arrest, the justice of the courtroom, and the pros or cons and presence or absence of diplomacy. Bringing in one international fugitive is always a multifaceted problem.

Another U.S. legal change has been the criminalizing of "material aid" to terrorist groups. This is a wedding of economic powers with law-making and enforcement. In pre-9/11 days in America and most democracies, a great deal of suspect activity escaped beneath the bar of what our laws regulated. Terrorist movements are political entities, which are often protected by our laws. Circumstances depending, one might before have legally sent medical aid, non-lethal supplies, money or other assistance to many violent political groups, yet not been questioned—let alone arrested. But beginning with the Clinton administration's executive acts barring material aid to a dozen Middle Eastern extremist groups, followed by formal changes in federal law achieved by Congress and the White House in 1995 and 1996, it is no longer viable to donate money and equipment and pretend to keep a proper distance from the bloody acts by the recipients. Resources are freely exchanged so that money given for bandages can be used to buy bullets; material aid of nearly all types to terrorists is now punishable in the United States.

"The Lackawanna Six" of the Buffalo metro area in New York State worked to aid Al Qaeda. Most of these Yemeni Americans trained together in the Al Faruq camp inside Afghanistan in the spring of 2001, where they met bin Laden. Given the laxity of those days, Immigration and Naturalization and other U.S. agencies knew little of these young men. But in a telling example of what citizens may do in their republic's defense, one concerned person, an Arab American, wrote a letter in somewhat shaky English to police, telling of this training trip and the youths' hopes for violent action. The letter called them "terrorists." An inquiry followed, and then arrests in New York and Bahrain, snuffing the hopes of this American terrorist cell. The charge under which they were convicted was materially supporting terrorism.[24] The same crime is the basis of the 2011 trial of Chicago citizen Tahawwur Rana, close friend of Mumbai massacre conspirator (and fellow-American) David Coleman Headley.[25]

The United States is not the only country to have changed its laws. Many countries have come online or are preparing to do so with new laws. This is due, in part, to a major reorientation at the United Nations. The UN is an international system of sovereign states, and during its first decades it hardly imagined controlling the flow of private monies to violent groups within individual nations. But in 2002 a new treaty mandated that all countries do exactly that. States are *required* to act against the financing of terrorism. Such an imperative from the UN had been suggested before 9/11, but only implemented afterwards.

Third, Congress passed the USA PATRIOT Act. Its long-winded name is "Uniting and Strengthening America by Providing Appropriate Tools Required to Intercept and Obstruct Terrorism." Of 535 Members of House and Senate, only 67 voted against it in late 2001. But war is a tiring business, and in subsequent years the act was challenged by some. Now that Osama bin Laden is dead, there will be choruses of unhappy voices at each interval when parts of the bill require renewal. In principle, there is nothing wrong with "sunset" legislation that only has effect for a set time, or during an emergency. The contention in this case is over whether to abandon surveillance and other powers that have helped to catch Al Qaeda members when that organization is very much alive, led by Ayman al Zawahiri and other veterans, and still making war on us.

Parts of the USA PATRIOT Act are ideas from Homeland Security Advisor Fran Townsend, the National Security Council's Richard Clarke, and other public servants during Bill Clinton's administration. Other parts were the work of a House and Senate in balance between the two parties. The law combines federal powers to access private credit card information and bank accounts, grants easier access to telephone taps and stored voice mails and e-mail, gives the right to "sneak and peak" search of a suspect's premises (with notification given to them only after the fact), and allows other intrusive means of finding terrorists. The principle of "probable cause" is preserved, and so is the principle of judicial oversight of the warrant process.

One provision stirred many librarians into dissent. They found it inappropriate that a suspect's book-borrowing record could be accessed, a concern anyone can understand. But a terrorist's education, and technical preparation, is one of the more revealing things about him or her. Unabomber Theodore Kaczynski's footnotes in his 35,000 word manifesto of 1995 helped his brother and the FBI to identify him after a 17-year hunt. If tomorrow the city of Seattle, or the township of Pennington, New Jersey, faced a crisis over a biological weapon made in a home laboratory, would it not be vital for police and the Center for Disease Control and others to know as much as humanly possible about the scientific sources the suspected maker of devil's brew had been using? Would those communities, or any other community, gripped by an epidemic *not* want police and medical authorities to know if the perpetrator had been using certain medical and scientific works at the library, or what he had accessed over publicly provided computer stations? Librarians' objections to releasing a list of borrowed books in such a rare case are a classic of the types of *kerfuffle* that roil us in peacetime; in a bio-crisis, virtually every citizen among us would *want* to aid the authorities' inquiry into what a terrorist had learned in our public libraries.

Another important provision in this congressional package is very much non-partisan; it is a measure that Democratic Congressmen favored in the 1990s when it was needed against domestic right-wingers and militiamen: the "roving wiretap." The provision makes modest concessions to refinements of modern communications in allowing police to get a legal order for a tap that applies to *all* the suspect's telephones. Since every watcher of television knows that a criminal can steal a cell phone, use a cell phone and throw it away in favor of a second, or rely upon public phones, it is obvious that to catch this individual, police should not have to fill a warrant request with every imaginable telephone number from which the suspect might dial. Incredibly, they did before 9/11. Under the USA PATRIOT Act, one warrant covers *any* phone the named suspect is using. Other traditional civil liberties strictures, such as probable cause and not listening in when the tapped line talk is purely personal, still protect the suspect.

Some provisions, such as those about financial records, are more aggressive and will always be subject to scrutiny. Their persistence in the law—or their disappearance in future years—will be part of a healthy public debate over balancing liberties of suspects and other citizens and the continuing threat of terrorist attacks. Our democracy will never be beyond the need of citizen and media scrutiny. Indeed, as respected a public servant as Robert Mueller, FBI director from 2001 to 2014, has publicly apologized for overuse of "National Security Letters"—a powerful system for acquiring records from businesses during investigations of individual terrorists. Their use peaked in 2005 when as many as 9,200 such letters were issued by the FBI pertaining to some 3,500 persons.[26]

There are other issues of law related to the fight against today's terrorism, including the crime of torture, which will be addressed in Part III. Of the final issues for consideration here, one is a matter of international law and another is of domestic law. These two problems needed addressing by the Obama administration and may well still, even after he is succeeded in the White House.

First, we are still at war, and "war" differs from "peace." The Obama administration opened in 2009 amidst good will and echoes of approval in the world community. President Obama—a law professor—is infrequently willing to call the fight with Al Qaeda "war." And yet he and his Justice Department have not come to grips with a divisive point: the difference between war and peace as it affects our courtrooms and our captives.

George W. Bush had declared that the Taliban (which in 2001 ruled most of Afghan territory) and Al Qaeda (the Taliban's ally and partner) presented a new form of warfare with too many gray areas for the lawyers. His White House eventually settled on according prisoner of war (POW) status to most Taliban fighters, but withholding that respected status from any international terrorist organization such as Al Qaeda. The Obama campaign demanded civil courts of law with their built-in elaborate protections for each suspect, something conservatives found ridiculous. This new strategy failed; few terrorists were brought to trial in 2009 to 2011, and in a 2010 case a known terrorist was convicted on only one count in the charged list of some 200 counts of murder. The public had every right to know what new direction would serve the new president. Nothing came. There was no fresh legal guideline and no new policy, apparently. Critics of the Bush administration continued surfacing official memos on harsh interrogations, but the public was not given a new path for properly trying or punishing terrorists. Eventually, early in 2011, the Justice Department led by Eric Holder and James Cole conceded that it could *not* try (most) Al Qaeda terrorists in civilian courts—that military commissions of the battlefield sort familiar throughout military history would serve for most cases. The whole has proven a muddle in which partisan politics have ousted political prudence. In the end the Obama team came around to the preceding Bush position allowing executive choice for civilian trials or military commissions.[27] That result will have to do: government should have options for trying terrorists, circumstances depending.

While that legal issue was intensively debated and never resolved, a second has gone largely ignored when it should have prompted discussion: the matter of an alien's difference from a full citizen of the United States. What is appropriate handling of a foreign terrorist caught on American territory, as opposed to a U.S. citizen caught performing the same act?

It is clear—and always has been—that Al Qaeda terrorists scorn the Geneva Accords and all other international laws of war meant to protect soldiers of legitimate armies. That is, terrorists do not wear uniforms, carry arms openly, respond to a recognized chain of command, or abstain from war crimes. Terrorists fight more like war criminals than legitimate uniformed combatants and thus deserve only the minimums: cool decency and protection from torture. Terrorists are owed little from international law tradition. Indeed, in some experts' views, international terrorists should be akin to pirates—who are classified as "enemies of humanity." Pirates can be, and should be, tried by any country that catches them: Somali pirates today face charges in Kenya, in Virginia, and a half-dozen other places. Jurisdiction in piracy cases is universal and has been since wise men first pondered protecting the international community by shaping international custom and law.

But the unmet challenge in our domestic law is the proper handling of aliens engaged in terrorism *here*, be they loners or members of a hostile foreign group, like the Al Qaeda members drifting around Florida, Virginia, Nevada, and New York during 2000 and 2001. Traditional American law did extend limited civil rights and due process to resident aliens. Yet, in recent decades, expansive court interpretations of the constitution have notably broadened aliens' rights. Compounding the errors of certain judges, Congress has added to this problem when writing new laws that cover all "persons" with the protections created earlier for our own "citizens."[28] Many media organizations perpetuate

the neglect of this vital distinction when writing righteous or indignant stories about the abuse of legal "rights" of some suspect who, one
learns only much later, is not American.

This lack of interest in citizenship is strange. Judicial and congressional decisions doubtless taken with a desire to respect and protect
the person who is "alien" in fact deprecate the status of all U.S. citizens. In some legal eyes, we now "owe" everyone and anyone the same
protections as an American citizen—though they may repudiate our
laws and principles.

The legal issues that could distinguish alien from citizen include
terms under which the court appoints an attorney, whether "Miranda
Rights" were read upon arrest, civil procedures such as "discovery" of
evidence pre-trial, and the like. An acute point is the use in court of
classified information. In national security affairs it is often the case
that sources and methods of intelligence must remain hidden or they
may be lost or stolen. If we insist upon presenting in open court that
an Al Qaeda "perp" was caught due to a special source—for example,
signals intelligence from his satellite phone—then Al Qaeda cadre still
in the field will cease using their satellite phones.[29] This is an immense
loss to our National Security Agency based at Fort Meade, Maryland,
expert at listening to such terrorist communications. One might reveal
this information in a military commission where "discovery" and
public access can be limited appropriately, while proceedings remain
impartial. One cannot do this in a normal civilian court.

Since 1978 we have had secretive courts—known as Foreign Intelligence Surveillance Act (FISA) Courts—in which special judges balance reasonable provisions for alien suspects with the need to protect
the U.S. FISA courts may be secret but they are for spies; terrorists
are not tried in them. Should there be such courts for alien terrorists,
so that evidence can be heard and weighed by a qualified judge, yet
the origins of this information go protected? Apparently the Clinton administration thought so: a domestic counterterrorism package
passed in 1996 provided for an "Alien Terrorist Removal Court," and
judges were appointed, but then no prosecutor had the audacity to use
it. Perhaps that court could be improved upon ... or at least tried.

Aliens who are in the United States to commit violent acts based
upon hostile ideologies should not be coddled and cuddled. Terrorism cases by their dangerous nature go far beyond the purse-snatch

victim, beyond the problem of many victims of a car theft ring, and go to the national security of all 315 million of us. Terrorism has that nature. Sources and methods of intelligence against terrorism are challenging to develop and they must be protected; open court proceedings designed for Americans deserving every possible protection are inappropriate. Yet, not only are we not fixing this problem—we are not even discussing it among ourselves. Perhaps citizens today fear that even using the old word "alien" is to mark one's self out as racist? In fact, legally specialized handling of alien terrorist suspects by U.S. courts would be a positive change, underscoring the privileges and responsibilities of full citizenship and an individual's part in the social contract that created the longest-living republic in human history.

## The Military

If force must be involved, the ideal counterterrorism action within a liberal democratic society would be exercised by police officers. As appropriate, a negotiator for hostage-barricade cases, or emergency response medical technicians or other experts, would be involved. Police have the lead in anticipating and countering terrorism. In many ways, having a military force in one of our cities is a very undesirable thing—no matter how good their training or how pure their motives. And, yet, the unfortunate truth, rammed home in modern democratic history in the United States, Western Europe, and other places, is that normal law enforcement personnel are not *always* sufficient to defeat terrorists' challenges.

Anarchism plagued European and U.S. cities a century ago, providing an early example of the *occasional* need for military reinforcement when terrorist firepower overmatches local policing. Anarchists had begun to terrify Londoners, as in the "Tottenham Outrage," shooting innocent passersby while escaping through city streets after a payroll robbery.[30] In 1911, several East European anarchists who had participated in another robbery holed up in an apartment building on Sidney Street in central London, mortally shooting a policeman who approached the door hoping to make an arrest. The terrorists' modern automatic pistols were devastating and their cartridge supply seemed bottomless. So authorities brought in an army platoon to back up the under-armed policemen collected from two city districts. What followed was an exchange of small arms fire that went on for hours and ended in the deaths of the two anarchists. The siege on Sidney Street seemed to have broken the spell these revolutionaries and nihilists had cast over the city. No such event was ever staged again by anarchists in London. The minister at the Home Office (the equivalent of our Justice Department) who supervised this response was a youthful Winston S. Churchill. He always felt that law—not just order—had been properly restored by this regrettable, short, controlled use of London police and military personnel.[31]

Especially during the last five decades, modern cities such as London have suffered instances in which local law enforcement is simply overwhelmed by a terrorist group's firepower or audacity. Our American cities have seen rioting that required outside help, from the racial affairs of Newark (answered by National Guard in 1967) to the case of heavily armed gangs in Los Angeles (answered by the Marines in 1992). No past case compares with the newest threats of contemporary terrorism. In Mumbai (Bombay), India, marauders with elaborate military training, and armed for a small war, tore the heart out of the city for 60 hours while local and central government floundered. Only later did the city establish the readiness and reallocation of specialized forces for a proper response on such an occasion.

Any one of America's mayors today could face the equivalent of Sidney Street's anarchists with machine pistols. We might think our own anarchists disappeared into high school history books. Yet, outside Cleveland in April 2012, five anarchists laid bombs under a bridge, hoping Highway 82 would collapse—something that could have taken many lives. In this case the FBI handled the matter; for nearly all others there are many levels of police who might suffice. But Mayor X, or City Council Chief Y, might face rioting spurred by another sort of terrorist group, with ill effects running quickly out of local control and requiring National Guardsmen. A single bio-attack would quickly outgrow all local authority. Our mayor might be confronted by a Mumbai scenario—a popular idea in the self-proclaimed "jihadi" world, which visualizes maximum lethal impact while downplaying escape by the shooters as irrelevant. There were many police on hand at Mumbai but they did not suffice. How tragic that it was after this attack, and not before, that India re-evaluated the availability and apportionment of its special response paratroops.

As terrorists master technology—and many have—federal assets are more important than ever because cities simply do not have or cannot afford some of the technical countermeasures that would be required. Any city mayor hosting a political spectacle or sports final may face security challenges outside the capabilities of his city police. The sponsorship of a foreign government could raise the threat presented by a criminal cartel or terrorist group far above the heads of normal response personnel, leaving them desperate for U.S. military assistance. Few metro areas could manage the crisis implicit in an attack with a truck of chlorine—already done several times in the Iraq war. If such an action were choking downtown Washington, D.C., it would be fully appropriate to call down from adjoining Maryland a competent military unit such as the "Chemical and Biological Incident Response Force" of the U.S. Marines. Aum Shinrikyo's sarin gas attack on underground trains in Tokyo might be copied. A well-organized municipal airport might need our Air National Guard, or its army counterpart, to respond to a sudden warning about a terror group with two or three shoulder-fired missiles.[32] In 2002 in Mombasa, Kenya, a chartered passenger plane saw two narrow misses during take-off; Al Qaeda was responsible. It is fortunate that these special capabilities are available to city mayors and state governors. It is just as fortunate that military interventions in our civic life are so rare and carefully limited by law and by the caution of elected authorities.

These and other such cases, hypothetical and actual, are classified as "military support to civil authorities," and all prudent democracies constrain them sharply. To return to London—where in several cases the Special Air Service (SAS) military force was used in terrorist cases—elaborate procedures control the "hand-off" from elected officials to a unit such the SAS. And the moment the crisis is resolved, the British military is compelled to, and eager to, hand back authority for the terrorist crime scene to locals, such as the MET, or Metropolitan Police.

In the United States, military support to civilian authorities includes the U.S. Northern Command, responsible for our defense from the northern tip of Alaska southward through Latin America. Liaison with Mexico and Canada is part of this command's daily business, and so are the national waters of the U.S., reaching out as far as 500 miles. NORTHCOM (U.S. Northern Command) oversees the military aircraft that check aviation threats such as 9/11—as well as defense against missiles. Yet in peacetime, it does not directly control the Coast Guard—which is a Department of Homeland Security entity. In unusual cases and places, very small, well-defined U.S. military forces also accomplish daily work for border security; the best example is Joint Task Force North (formerly JTF Six) on the Mexican line, where military sensors and helicopters are especially useful for the "low-intensity conflict" that has long characterized that 1,900 mile border.

Our military forces also defend this homeland from overseas. A fundamental principle of national strategy is that we defend the homeland on distant ramparts,[33] rather than having the fight come to Main Street. September 2001 showed a clear failure in this respect. It occurred, in part, because during three previous decades it was the practice of terrorists to hit Americans overseas, rather than at home. It was easier then, and still is easier, to attack U.S. citizens abroad. Thus, our men and women in uniform overseas practice "force protection" but are also involved in innumerable other exercises and operations to deter and prevent terrorists and states alike from striking our people, our bases, our infrastructure, and our homeland.

The U.S. pre-positions assets abroad (at sea and on land) for use when the time comes without having to move them there in a hurry at great cost in time. It keeps important bases alive and humming in spots such as Manas, Kyrgyzstan, and Daegu, Korea. The Unted States invests in well-distributed listening posts. It keeps fighter, bomber, and transport aircraft at the ready, and flies unmanned aerial vehicles (UAVs) out of Incirlik in Turkey, Naimey in Niger, Sigonella in Sicily, etc. Our air force has special operations aircraft and personnel stationed at Mildenhall, England, Cannon Air Force Base, New Mexico, and Kadena, Japan, among other places.[34] Americans work with allies on missile defense against rogue states that have both missiles and a record of terrorism sponsorship. The rogues include North Korea, Syria, and Iran.[35] Our allies include Japan, the Republic of Korea, Australia, the United Kingdom, and Israel. In early 2013 Israel enjoyed yet another successful test of missile interceptors; its "Arrow 3" is the product of long domestic effort and collaboration with U.S. experts.

Our infantry have been involved in continuous low-level wars related only in limited ways to our global fight against terrorism. These military forces are not more important to the effort than our many types of police, in the perspective of grand strategy. But their impressive and sometimes exhausting service has been important to the lives of a whole generation. In Afghanistan (from late 2001) and Iraq (from spring 2003), U.S. troops by the tens of thousands have fought counterinsurgency wars. Their enemies—often complex entities that fight in hybrid forms of warfare—include terrorists who target civilians; guerrillas who attack our military infrastructure and armed personnel; and insurgents, intimate with many in the local population and building political support for their own visions of the future. The Taliban is an example of an insurgent force that is equally at home with terrorist or guerrilla tactics and also runs its own "shadow government" in many parts of Afghanistan. This group's partnership with Al Qaeda—which assigned hundreds of its fighters to the Taliban's army in the late 1990s—led George W. Bush to order the invasion of Afghanistan in late 2001 to crush both Taliban and Al Qaeda. A Republican White House made that choice, the war was won quickly, and a Democratic candidate and President Barak Obama spoke out approvingly of that war. Citizens can judge: there are no training camps in Afghanistan producing new Al Qaeda bombers and pilots. It is less clear what will come once we withdraw from most of Afghanistan in 2014.[36]

Iraq has been a very different experience. It was a haven for several key Palestinian terrorists, one of whom was captured when U.S. forces arrived. Iraq was home to many other international extremists, but only a very few of the Al Qaeda sort.[37] It was not Al Qaeda but other factors, such as decades on the State Department's list of sponsors of terror, reports of chemical weaponry, and Iraq's flagrant disobedience of UN sanctions, that most pulled the White House into that second theater in March 2003—for good or ill. The Obama administration has completed the gradual withdrawal planned by its predecessor, but also led us into a third and a fourth engagement: Libya and Syria. These last two limited wars began with little relation to terrorism but tied to the future of North Africa and its governance.

The open and large-scale wars in Afghanistan and Iraq were thus related to the fight against international terrorism in complicated ways. RAND scholar Brian Jenkins has aptly termed them interrelated campaigns, all going on simultaneously, rather than one single "war." Among the most important realities of the fighting is this: if we lose any of these contests and an ugly new regime emerges, we could face future terrorist threats from the new host. That risk, and our burdensome national debt and other domestic factors, are all in play as decisions are made by the president, his national security staff, and Congress.

A dramatically lower scale of U.S. military force is visible in discrete and short-term operations that sting or seize a precise enemy. The objective may be to destroy encampments, capture terrorists, kill an elusive enemy, or do all of these as appropriate to the mission, in a war zone or in peacetime. The SEAL Team Six experts from the U.S. Navy who killed Osama bin Laden on May 1, 2011 are sons of a powerful U.S. patriarch, the Special Operations Command, which grew in prominence throughout the 1980s and 1990s, and yet again after 2001. No other dimension of our military has enjoyed such growth. Citizens, politicians, and generals alike seem to admire this national creation, grown out of small programs such as the Green Berets of the Vietnam era, and Delta Force created in the decade after the 1972 Munich Olympics massacre. They have also developed their own intelligence capabilities and can thus operate overseas, independent and quiet, liaising as appropriate with host-country specialists.

Specialized military forces have expanded dramatically yet kept all their good qualities. These highly skilled and well-practiced personnel are ready and trained to deal with airline hijacking, enemy capture of a ship, or an embassy crisis involving hostages, among other terrorist scenarios. Some have seen tactical action in the Arabian Sea since piracy increased, as in rescuing Captain Richard Phillips of the cargo ship *Maersk Alabama* in 2009, killing several Somali pirates in the process. But at home in the United States, most crises can and should be handled by the appropriate combination of FBI (with its Hostage Rescue Teams and other capabilities), state, and local police forces, perhaps using their Special Weapons and Tactics (SWAT) teams. Acting on a tip in mid-1997, New York City's finest broke into the Brooklyn apartment of two Palestinians building nail bombs to use in the city subway. Despite several past deportations, the pair had re-entered the United States through Canada and were moving quickly with this plot. A loyal citizen informed against them. The terrorists resisted with firearms when police burst in but both were subdued. The case did not linger long in our headlines for an important and encouraging reason:

in almost every domestic case involving terrorists in the United States, including Al Qaeda men, arrests have occurred *without* killing. There is much good to be said for the skills of the officers involved. Unlike their predecessors of 1930 or 1960, these men and women in blue are increasingly trained and knowledgeable about terrorists and how they may differ from the usual criminals.

Two summary points are appropriate before leaving this brief on our military's varied roles in countering terrorism. One is to note a marked increase in the limited ways in which national intelligence assets and military forces work together. They always have, but only to a degree. They came closer after a searching review of incidences of non-cooperation during the first Gulf War of 1991. Now, we often see senior military officers holding high posts in our intelligence organizations. The last decade has seen remarkable enhancements in this interaction, illustrated by their co-direction of the drone campaign against insurgent groups and terrorist leaders. President Obama has redoubled, and redoubled again, the harsh work of President Bush in this use of guided but pilotless small aircraft. The results are impressive, precise, and much less dangerous to U.S. personnel than Special Forces raids, and less expensive for our nation. Our military forces are thus performing better overseas.

At home, too, the different levels of U.S. actors prepared and trained to use force against terrorism have become better integrated and more cooperative. While our movie screens still play up turf fights separating U.S. entities, in practice there is evidence of progress. Despite resistance, and legacies of rivalry, our uniformed services learned to work together in the last quarter century; now such organizations as the CIA Directorate of Operations, the military services, the FBI, and state and local police are also getting ever more used to terms such as "fusion" and "joint." It was not always so. It is better today.[38] For domestic U.S. agencies to perform at this high level will always demand that the executives in these different but related U.S. agencies be ready to reach across the aisle, the street, and the jungle pathway to offer a collegial hand. Bureaucratic selfishness is the bane of counterterrorism.

## Notes

1 Daniel Benjamin, a National Security Council veteran, became Obama's ambassador-at-large on counterterrorism at the State Department (until

December 2012). He pressed for less use of the term "terrorism" and more use of the phrase "violent extremism," indicating the latter was the current American enemy. While governmental usage did change, the present author does not think it an improvement.

2   Aaron Danis of the National Counterterrorism Center recalls how "the 4 Ds" were developed by military officers studying at National Defense University; from their points arose the architecture of the first national U.S. strategy for combating terrorism (2003).

3   For example, at a very good June 2011 conference at the U.S. Institute of Peace in Washington, D.C., no speaker denied that governments often do talk to, and make deals with, terror groups. Panelists thought the more useful question is when and how one might responsibly and effectively conduct such talks.

4   Interview with the author, Ambassador Robert G. Joseph, *Countering WMD: The Libyan Experience* (Fairfax, VA: National Institute Press, 2009).

5   White House, *National Strategy for Counterterrorism* (2011), 16: www.whitehouse.gov.

6   Phil Peters, formerly a staff expert on Central America for Congressman James A. Courter (Republican, NJ) and now an officer of The Lexington Institute, Arlington, Virginia, at work on Cuban affairs; telephone interview with the author, 2006.

7   MILF's treaty had collapsed in August 2011, but peace was resurrected and affirmed by signatures a year later, announced the *Washington Post* of October 8, 2012. The communist New People's Army is left as the main enemy in the field for Filipinos. But there was trouble with an MNLF Faction in 2013 also.

8   Bill Clinton, regarded as a master politician, made enormous efforts on the Middle East peace question in his last years as president. Talks at the Wye River resort in Maryland were one part of these. There was no breakthrough.

9   See, for example, Mark Perry, *Talking to Terrorists: Why America Must Engage with its Enemies* (New York: Perseus, 2010).

10  These cases appear in the 2nd edition of my book *Terrorism Today* (2007). On Abu Sayyaf hostage-taking, see Roberto N. Aventajado, *140 Days of Terror: In the Clutches of the Abu Sayyaf* (Pasig City, Philippines: Anvil, 2003).

11  There are two other major factors for the current success; see *Orbis* (Fall, 2012), 588–607, "Spain's ETA Terrorist Group is Dying."

12  Lecturing at the Institute of World Politics in Washington about 2004, a veteran of the FBI reviewed that case, including the rendition, conducted with Pakistani help.

13  "Back on September 11, terrorists attacked our metropolitan cores, two of America's great cities. They did that because they knew that was where they could do the most damage and weaken us the most," O'Malley said. "Years later, we are given a budget proposal by our commander in chief, the president of the United States. And with a budget ax, he is attacking America's cities. He is attacking our metropolitan core." *Washington Post*, February 9, 2005.

14  Christopher C. Harmon, "Sudan's Neighbors Accuse It of Training Terrorists: Egypt, Algeria, and Israel are Among Those Angered at Khartoum's Furnishing of Bases for Teaching Assassins," *Christian Science Monitor*, December

19, 1995. Though seeing the problem of Sudanese aid to international terror, I did not know of Osama bin Laden's presence there.

15 Evidence of this includes a recommendation by a former Secret Service officer to see "Is It Real, Or Super K?" in *Newsweek*, June 9, 1996. North Korean counterfeit bills have been circulated by a Japanese communist terrorist, among others.

16 *Country Reports on Terrorism: 2009*, 265.

17 Central Asian graduate students have complained to me of this. One British commentary on the problem is by Seumas Milne in *The Guardian* on October 13, 2005.

18 Those not interested in reading the entire act may see the précis by the Congressional Research Service, "The USA PATRIOT Act: A Sketch," April 18, 2002.

19 To my account of events and their significance, colleague Aaron Danis adds a link from the Harvard J. F. K. School of Government that includes the Younis case, among several: http://www.hks.harvard.edu/research/publications/terrorism.htm. An authoritative explanation of "The Long Arm of the Law" by the Department of Justice appears under that name in the FBI's annual *Terrorism in the United States: 1997* (Washington, D.C.: GPO, 1998), 14–15.

20 From Milan in 2003, and from a German locale in 2004, individuals were rendered out by U.S. teams, whose clumsiness reportedly exposed their identities (e.g., *Washington Post*, February 2, 2007).

21 FBI, *Terrorism in the United States: 1997*, 14–15. See also these terms of art, briefly but formally worded, in *Black's Law Dictionary*. "Rendition" is returning a fugitive to the country where he faces legal charges. "Extraordinary rendition" usually means doing so without formal legal approval, perhaps by covert action. In both cases the suspect faces legal proceedings in a place where he has been charged with a crime. Former Foreign Service Officer Leonard Hill told the author in a Washington, D.C., interview in late May 2011 of a past case of a quiet rendition of a terrorist suspect from Belize. Hill served our embassy there. Because the suspect was deemed dangerous and had broken immigration law in entering Belize, that country was pleased to put him onto an American airplane and see him flown out. For Belize, this resolved a knotty problem in one day, and almost invisibly; they found it better than trying the man in court.

22 See, for example, "Terrorist Renditions 1987–1999," in the FBI's *Terrorism in the United States: 1999; 30 Years of Terrorism; A Special Retrospective Edition* (Washington, D.C.: GPO, undated), 52.

23 *Carlos*, a 2010 film over five hours' long and directed by Oliver Assaya, released in The Criterion Collection.

24 Dina Temple-Raston, *The Jihad Next Door: The Lackawanna Six and Rough Justice in the Age of Terror* (New York: Public Affairs, 2007). She reports well for National Public Radio on domestic U.S. terrorism.

25 The November 2008 tragedy in Mumbai left just one gunman alive. But others contributed to the 60-hour rampage, probably including Pakistanis of the ISI and two Americans (*Washington Post*, May 23, 2011).

26  The *Washington Post* broke the story of the use of the letters on May 2, 2006. Stories on federal surveillance in such ways appeared in the *New York Times* (May 3) and the *Washington Times* (May 4). Subsequent articles appeared on surveillance in the *New York Times* in 2006. See also Graff, *Threat Matrix*, 503–504.

27  What does still distinguish the two administrations is the Obama team's fierce opposition to anything it considers torture, including water-boarding.

28  These lines about aliens and our law were aided by an interview with Dr. John Eastman, professor of constitutional law, February 9, 2004. This paragraph resembles one in my Heritage Foundation *Backgrounder* no. 1760 (May 19, 2004)—the first English-language publication to deal at length with "How Al Qaeda May End?" Thanks are due to Jim Phillips of The Heritage Foundation and to Williamson Murray, editing a book for Cambridge University Press, for their early interest in this work creating a conceptual structure for many cases of how older terrorist groups *did* end. One of the networks studied was of violent 19th-century anarchists.

29  In 1998, writes Porter Goss, later a director of the CIA, a newspaper note about the U.S. tracking of bin Laden's satellite phone caused discontinuation of that habit and loss of priceless intelligence: "Loose Lips Sink Spies," *New York Times*, February 10, 2006. Also in 2006, the *New York Times* published a "scoop" about Belgium-based snooping into international banking records; this became a public debate matter and was dangerous for the effort against terrorists.

30  This is the identical neighborhood where a century later, in August 2011, mindless rampages broke out and then spread to other parts of London.

31  "Anarchism and Fire: What We Can Learn from Sidney Street," author's essay in *Finest Hour*, no 150 (Spring, 2011). Churchill said in another context in 1926: "I decline utterly to be impartial as between the fire brigade and the fire." *Churchill by Himself: The Definitive Collection of Quotations*, ed. Richard Langworth (New York: Public Affairs, 2008), 402.

32  There is an imminent threat to commercial air travel worldwide from shoulder-fired missiles. They are sophisticated, cheap (relative to, say, a nuclear bomb), made in many countries, and attractive to terrorists for delivering a mass lethality incident. Three dozen commercial airplanes have been attacked with these weapons, including shoot-downs of commercial aircraft in Africa and Asia. See my table of "Attacks by MANPAD Missiles" at pages 109–110 of *Terrorism Today* (2nd edition).

33  Harold W. Rood, "Distant Rampart," *U.S. Naval Institute Proceedings*, March (1967), 30–37.

34  Fred J. Pushies, *U.S. Air Force Special Ops* (St. Paul, MN: MBI, 2007).

35  See *America at Risk: The Citizen's Guide to Missile Defense* by James H. Anderson, then of The Heritage Foundation in Washington, D.C. (1999). His book initiated my own thoughts about the need for one on terrorism and counterterrorism.

36  The October 2012 Vice Presidential Debate made it evident that both American parties support withdrawal from Afghanistan.

37 The question of Iraq's relationship to international terrorism was contentious during the G. W. Bush administration, and excesses came from both political sides. Mr. Bush's White House tied the March 2003 invasion of Iraq to the larger "Global War on Terrorism," while many analysts and citizens suspected they were after Saddam Hussein and "unfinished business" of the first Gulf War. The White House in 2003 also stressed other causes for action: the dangers of WMD; Iraqi flaunting of the oil embargo; and Saddam's disdain for one UN Security Council resolution after another.

Certain Al Qaeda personnel had been in contact or taken training in Iraq, and evidence of such contacts *may* be "Case Closed," an article allegedly based on a Defense Department document in the *Weekly Standard* of November 24, 2003. But the best-known terrorists present in Iraq before the war were unrelated to Al Qaeda: Abu Abbas and Abu Nidal, Palestinians. These and others with Iraqi links were forgotten in the public discourse, amid assertions that "there was no link between Iraq and terrorism." There *was*. Iraq had a place on the State Department's list of state sponsors of terrorism *for three decades*, with one year's exception. Pariah status for Iraq ended after Saddam fell to the coalition.

38 Military officers often speak of applying their familiar model, the Goldwater–Nichols Act that revamped the Pentagon and some civil–military relations in 1986, to coerce varied federal agencies into better working relationships. See, for example, the work of Matthew Bogdanos, a reservist and colonel of marines.

# 5

# THE PUBLISHED COUNTERTERRORISM STRATEGY

In theory, all the elements of national power discussed above should be combined in an overall national approach. Diplomacy is an alternative preferable to force, but at times it must support the threat and use of force. U.S. military power in a troubled region where we have been asked to help may be a stabilizing factor that inhibits insurgency for that partner country. Economic inducements should underscore diplomacy. Foreign Service officers should explain U.S. military deployments to overseas audiences with the same adeptness that they present cultural ambassadors or lay out new programs of foreign aid. And the federal government should, in some limited cases, aid states and localities in countering terrorism—even as communities themselves grow more alert to their security needs in an era of "self-radicalized" would-be martyrs with guns. So, a grand strategy would have all these elements of national power working together. Do they? How good is our master plan?

A *National Strategy for Counterterrorism* was published by the White House in June 2011. Accessible on the Internet at www.white-house.gov, it need not be quoted at length here, but this document deserves a close reading.[1] Admittedly, it is not seen by many U.S. citizens ... few federal documents are. Those who do study the 19 pages may not find them candid about the real problems we Americans face in the fight with terrorists; not many federal documents are fully candid. Of the readers who do take the time, many—inside and outside Washington—may feel unsatisfied.

The document would have us "disrupt, degrade, and discredit" terrorists and their organizations. It twice asserts the intention to "defeat" Al Qaeda and its affiliates—making an alliterative foursome of the letter "D." It emphasizes stolid, correct responses to acts of terror that do occur—which is called "resilience." To excessive degrees it counts on multilateral aid—though foreign partners rarely have our level of vigilance about our interests and our lives. There is only passing mention of "deterring" terrorists—the administration rightly sees few options for such a strategy against the fanatics in Al Qaeda.[2] The June 2011 strategy also briefly surveys the major U.S. opponents in the terror underground and those fighting U.S. interests in ongoing insurgencies. President Obama's strategy argues that we must have high principles guide our efforts in countering terrorism—language clearly intended as contrast with earlier scandals over torture and the Abu Ghraib prison in Iraq.

Apart from the moralism—which is always needed—there are few "new" ideas in the new strategy. That paucity suggests that we have learned less than we should about our enemies and how to beat them during so many years of fighting Al Qaeda. Counterterrorism specialists will recognize many ideas of the last administration, pulled forward for continued good service but without imaginative turns or enhancements. (Even the idea of "4 Ds" was used by the preceding White House strategy.) Those who believe we have been poor players in the field of "public diplomacy" will not even find that phrase in the latest *National Strategy for Counterterrorism*. There are too many exhortations to improve our image abroad, yet almost no ideas on how to do that. The reader with expectations that a "national strategy" against terrorists will surely set out approaches to "political warfare" will not find those words either.

A citizen concerned by the muddle about civilian court trials for Al Qaeda fanatics, or a lawyer specializing in such matters, will see in the new paper demands for "an effective, durable legal framework for CT [counterterrorist] operations and bringing terrorists to justice." That is desirable, and must be part of any grand strategy, but it is not what we have. The White House has also issued no clarification of how standing international laws of war bear on the Al Qaeda fight. A recent commander of U.S. troops in Afghanistan, Marine General John Allen, told Congress in his confirmation hearing that if he caught an Al Qaeda man outside of a recognized war zone, he would not be sure how to jail him appropriately in advance of a required military hearing or civilian trial. The Justice Department's political appointees have merely reversed themselves—when what is needed is strong indication about the new path.

President Obama's counterterrorism document also lacks candor. We expect candor and are even told we require it: "Wherever and whenever possible, the United States will make information available to the American people about the threats we face and the steps being taken to mitigate those threats. A well-informed American public is a source of our strength." But in other paragraphs of this same *National Strategy for Counterterrorism*, opportunities for informing the American citizens are lost. Three examples will suffice.

U.S. citizens know that Pakistan was at best grotesquely negligent, at worst conniving, about Osama bin Laden's long residence in Abbottabad, a village near Pakistan's military academy. Many Americans also know that senior Taliban leaders live semi-openly in Pakistan, even as our men and women combat Taliban gunmen in Afghanistan. But there is no admission in the strategy paper of the scope of this "Pakistan problem." Neither the mess, nor a solution, is visible in the document. Military aid to that capital should have been deeply cut, with its possible restoration used as a diplomatic lever; but neither that nor any other strategic option is mentioned. Leaving office, Chairman of the Joint Chiefs of Staff Admiral Michael Mullen directly spoke out against Pakistan's official connections to both Taliban and the Haqqani network[3] in Afghanistan—both had killed Americans in that country. Was the 2011 counterterrorism strategy—released just about that time—so much less forthright than the admiral because the administration does not know what to do about Pakistan?

Second, it seems that the authors of the 2011 strategy want us to think Al Qaeda is nearly beaten. While a few words say otherwise, most of the document *does* tend in this direction. The published strategy must direct our inter-agency efforts against terrorists, not just prepare us for defense budget cuts that citizens knew were impending. Two times the strategy document reports that bin Laden is dead and was "the only leader Al Qaeda has ever known." Those words ignore the collective character of the organization, founded with a *shura* council—a kind of Islamist politburo. Such words ignore Ayman al Zawahiri, who was a close partner of bin Laden (and his personal physician) for a quarter-century, and before that had run his own Egyptian terrorist group. His Al Jihad merged formally into Al Qaeda just before 9/11 and Al Zawahiri assumed the number two post. He has long been leading and educating Al Qaeda personnel; his video and written production always exceeded bin Laden's; today he holds the top job in Al Qaeda. And several high-ranking veterans on Al Qaeda's staff are Egyptians like Zawahiri, especially Saif al Adel, whose picture is in the first book published[4] in America about Al Qaeda. Therefore, the new national document errs in giving the impression that Al Qaeda is rudderless.

A third way the document lacks candor is subtle. It is in the shifting of careful words related to a very important question: what is the end state of this fight? After so many years of war, when will our citizenry know we have done enough or have, perhaps, won? One answer could be when the top leaders of Al Qaeda and its affiliates are captured or killed, and when the ideology that radicalizes new cadre is intellectually and spiritually discredited. Another possible answer was proposed by the George W. Bush administration: the 2003 strategy promised to carry on until "the threat of terrorist attacks does not define our daily lives." Those words indicated an ongoing and full engagement. What a contrast in *meaning* with similar words is the newer (2011) document: "we have placed our counterterrorism campaign in a context that does not dominate the lives of the American people ... ." This means that *we have not won, yet we are easing back, favoring other priorities, and not demanding much of the citizen.* Here, again, within the current policy, are similar words: "our citizens have not let the specter of terrorism disrupt their daily lives ... ." This effectively means not that we are fighting and winning, as a nation, but that we can let the army do the work. Little wonder that some of our deployment-worn military brethren now summarize civil–military relations with the wise-crack that "We fight everywhere, while back home, people go to the mall."

The *National Strategy for Counterterrorism* which Obama published does not explicitly renounce any of the earlier White House goals. Its language is notably less martial—beginning with its title, which calls for "countering" terrorism and not "combating" it as the Bush administration pronounced. There is also appropriate emphasis upon a "whole of government" approach. These two differences appeal to the U.S. allies who have felt that the U.S. strategy has been too military. The Obama document emphasizes multilateral action—an approach some citizens cannot associate with G. W. Bush, but an approach that is prudent in a world of multilateral terrorist organizations.

There is a sound continuity in both administrations' strategy papers about weapons of mass destruction. All recent strategy papers maintain the strong sense of all presidents, beginning with William J. Clinton, that the nexus between terrorism and WMD is a pressing reason that terrorism can be incredibly dangerous. This may well explain why President Obama still says, on rare occasions, that we remain "at war" with the Al Qaeda network and its affiliates. But more generally there is some cheery news in the Obama national strategy against terrorism: for example, its timing meant that he could welcome news of the 2010 "Arab Spring" and the 2011 death of Osama bin Laden—two reasons that Americans sleep somewhat better at night than during the previous decade.

The continuing challenge for each administration is to carry on the good counterterrorist work on many fronts, while also watching for new opportunities and new ideas. So, what else should be done?

## Notes

1 This White House document made for a lengthy discussion with host Derrick T. Dortch of Federal News Radio (Washington, D.C.), July 15, 2011; the station archives such programs, with access online.

2 While social science and think tank communities have invested much time in recent years in studies of deterrence regarding Al Qaeda, they have been unable to make viable recommendations for such a strategy. Classic deterrence theory, an academic pursuit in the United States since the nuclear arms race, appears to be of little help in understanding or dealing with Islamist cells and radical individuals and Al Qaeda Central.

3 Jalaluddin Haqqani takes his last name from Darul Uloom Haqqania, a religious school in Pakistan where he studied. He became a Taliban minister in Afghanistan and has been a mix of guerrilla leader, terrorist, and organized criminal.

4 Yonah Alexander of The Potomac Institute has vast experience with terrorism issues. His book co-authored with Michael Swetnam showed the face of Saif al Adel—and, of course, the face of Ayman al Zawahiri—in a small gallery called "The Organizational Structure," in *Usama bin Laden's Al Qaeda: Profile of a Terrorist Network* (Ardsley, NY: Transaction Publishers, September 2001).

# Part III
# THE FUTURE

# 6

# WHAT NEEDS TO BE DONE

The last chapter ended with notes of careful criticism of the published U.S. strategy for countering terrorism. We all need to better understand this fight and under-gird our will for it, and our public officials must retool some U.S. strategies and hunt up novel concepts. It is just as vital that citizens, politicians framing questions for electoral races, commentators, and academics know about the many things the United States is doing right against world terrorism. America does *not* need a counterterrorist "revolution." Nor do we need to ramp up the counterterrorism budget—this fight, due to its nature, is cheaper and more limited than most counterinsurgency or conventional war.[1] Deficits and the national debt debate need not threaten counterterrorism efforts.

There are innumerable successes and successful programs underway, and at least a few deserve noting. Several years before the heat of the current discussions of cyber war, the United States created a new and forward-looking U.S. Cyber Command at Fort Meade, Maryland, where the National Security Agency can support its worldwide intelligence requirements. The command is increasingly able to counter extremists' and hackers' attacks on our infrastructure. If permitted, it can attack terrorist nets that wage cyber war on the United States and its allies. It can coordinate American efforts with allies' efforts—such as the operational and promising center for cyber defense in Estonia, run by NATO. Much of counterterrorism turns upon good intelligence, and ours is improved. Compared with a decade ago, we now have more human sources, equally adept technical sources, and better "fusion" of all sources. The Federal Bureau of Investigation has evolved into an intelligence organization, adding to its traditional role as an agency for law enforcement.

Despite many plots, there has been no Al Qaeda-<u>directed</u> bloody success here in over a decade. Our intelligence services and military forces have killed or captured so many junior and mid-level Al Qaeda operatives and commanders that aspiring to be *the* senior military commander is now the most dangerous job on our planet. No sooner had newspapers of May 2011 speculated that the 45-year-old Pakistani terrorist Ilyas Kashmiri might take that post, the papers of the next month brought word of his death in a U.S. drone attack.[2] A top Al Qaeda Central operator from Libya named Atiyah abd al-Rahman was also killed in August 2011. The next month saw a drone strike kill two of the most effective Al Qaeda propagandists in the world, a pair of Americans resident in Yemen and responsible for *INSPIRE* magazine.[3] Part of our national effort is to break the links between the various Al Qaeda franchises—what David Kilcullen calls a strategy of "dis-articulation." The United States and its allies *have* boxed in or chopped back certain Al Qaeda affiliates. Filipinos, with American help, have decimated Abu Sayyaf terrorist strength. Some groups in Iraq, Al Shabab, and several other affiliates of Al Qaeda, have not been contained. The international picture on nuclear proliferation is improved; the program named for former Senators Sam Nunn (Democrat, Georgia) and Richard Lugar (Republican, Indiana) monitors and restricts nuclear materials; smuggling of nuclear materials is way down. Al Qaeda probably lacks the money now to purchase a bomb, and even if it has, it might not be able to move its money to close a sale. That leaves lesser forms of nuclear attack conceivable and possible; but the risks of an Al Qaeda mass lethality nuclear attack are diminished today. And, finally, international organizations are helping our strategists and combatants. The United Nations and Interpol—both of which used to disdain anti-terrorist action—are finally moving, and they are tracking better with Washington. Over time, both of these powerful international actors will have good effects on international opinion and coordinated action.

But this is not enough. Al Qaeda is not beaten.

Ayman al Zawahiri has command. Noted affiliates around the world have pledged loyalty to him. The current *National Strategy for Counterterrorism* is misleading in presenting bin Laden as "the only leader Al Qaeda has ever known" and "the most influential advocate for attacking the United States ... ." Dr. Al Zawahiri has had a powerful role in those respects and held the formal number 2 leadership role for a decade until bin Laden was killed. If Zawahiri is now captured or killed, operational commander Saif al Adel[4] and certain other senior Al Qaeda cadre are still at large. The death of bin Laden did not seem to discourage many Al Qaeda fanatics—nor would it, logically speaking, since they avow that they love martyrdom. We see no new surrenders or apparent defections ... which are *the* most telling signs that a terrorist group or larger insurgency is beaten.

It is dangerous and illusory to think that this war died with Osama bin Laden in 2011. As a comparison, a U.S. citizen may see a limited parallel with the mid-point of World War II in Europe. The death by hanging of Benito Mussolini in mid-1943 meant the steep decline of "fascism," which he had introduced to Europe (and even to Adolf Hitler). The hanging by Italian partisans meant a dramatic difference in the Allies' war in Italy. But war was not over: there would be two more years of very hard work before Germany and Austria could be beaten, as they had their own reasons for fighting. Clearly, our fight with Al Qaeda Central is a far more limited, easier war than what Franklin Roosevelt and the United States faced. But we remain at war and, moreover, we are contesting an international movement, not merely a vanguard group. Consider the fighting in Yemen. Consider that the Taliban insurgency is unbeaten, killing Coalition soldiers, and swelled with both success and masses of cash from the opium business.[5]

America has a mandate for action. Common sense, ancient principles, innumerable world leaders, and United Nations Security Council resolutions have forcefully condemned terrorism generally[6] and Al Qaeda in particular. What should we continue, and what new enhancements or changes are required for the fight?

Our objective is to defeat and destroy Al Qaeda Central, both its personnel and its Islamist ideological appeal—for both are centers of strength. As the vanguard leads an international Islamist network, our coalition should continue its work dividing and containing Al Qaeda's affiliates and support structures. This combination would go far toward breaking apart the unofficial Militant Islamist International. At minimum, we must battle Al Qaeda as long as Al Zawahiri is at large, and so long as the group's doctrine remains strong enough to

regenerate top-grade cadre. Fighting that evil doctrine via ideological struggle is an objective the Bush and Obama administrations have
often recognized but rarely contested well.

Meanwhile, our offensive and defensive efforts against state sponsors of terrorists, as well as sub-state non-Islamist groups, must carry
on in accord with our established national principle of opposing *all*
terrorism as illegitimate. Study of international relations makes it evident that, as of the late 1960s, terrorism is now a tool of policy for
some. Terrorism will never be eliminated, any more than all crime
can be stopped in Detroit or Los Angeles. But as terrorism is, by definition, an attack on a whole polity, it must be brought down to the
lowest manageable levels, to a point at which it no longer poisons our
daily lives with fear. Historically speaking, "war" against terrorism is
not usually required; our current phase of martial effort will not last
indefinitely. But it is equally clear that, in counterterrorism, continuous effort is required, and sometimes so, too, is occasional use of force
by police or the military, or an ally's power.

Who is in charge of the counterterrorism fight? The president and
the executive branch of government direct U.S. efforts. Multifaceted
efforts, coordinated with domestic U.S. and foreign partners, are
required if we are to have good grand strategy for countering terrorism. That places our National Security Council—recently often called
the National Security Staff— in a central spot. Working intimately
with the executive power, and taking the president's lead, the NSC
should be at the center of decision-making in a "whole of government"
approach. Despite occasional fits of criticism, there is no need to dump
the NSC merely because it was established in the late 1940s, an era
not plagued with international terrorism. Nor is there need for separate wings of the NSC devoted, respectively, to "homeland" affairs
and "foreign" affairs. The council was designed to deal with both—
and domestic terrorism is all too often connected to the international
brands. NSC staff numbers hover between 100 and 200 "policy"
people and should thus prove adaptable and flexible and responsive
and under close White House control. They should begin by preparing a short document—to be made public—that clearly establishes
what executive agencies have which "leads" in countering what kinds
of terrorism. Cyber, financial, ideological, and other types of terrorism are hybrid threats; a single executive agency should have, and be

responsible for, leading that U.S. government effort on that problem. The president and his NSC must sensibly allocate these responsibilities and then lead, push, and sometimes shove to get action.

More specifically, the following are some points of emphasis for renewing our national counterterrorist effort in the years 2014, 2015, and beyond.

## Deny Terrorists Their Sanctuaries

In both geographic and "virtual" worlds, international terrorism continues to enjoy refuge. The problem begins with weak, lackadaisical, or indulgent foreign governments. In gray areas such as parts of Yemen, North Africa, and obscure parts of Southwest Asia, training camps and safe-havens of terrorism persist. Baluchistan, a complex and tumultuous area of Pakistan, has contributed many individuals to world terrorism: in 1993 alone, one killer from this region shot employees of the Central Intelligence Agency in Langley, Virginia, while others truck bombed the south tower of the World Trade Center. Washington must engage more strongly with the national governments of such countries. First, we should press them harder to do adequate frontier and internal policing, in accord with their duty and sovereignty, to not let terrorists pass their borders. Second, we should deny or supply assistance in ways explicitly and directly tied to better local performance in the security sector and in general governance. "No performance? No aid!" When foreign aid is appropriate and flowing, it can help to accomplish what Washington calls "capacity-building," the equivalent of teaching a man to fish for himself. Capacity-building in foreign security sectors, while difficult and slow, can be one of the smarter things we do to help our own security overseas and here at home.

Another type of sanctuary is offered by fully willing states rather than countries marred by shoddy and underperforming governments. Iran and Syria grant sanctuary and political offices to Palestinians and Lebanese of Hezbollah. In the current war in Syria, Lebanese Shia and Hezbollah enthusiastically back the regime of Bashar al Assad even though it is for them too secular in character, "apostate" in deliberately neglecting most of Islamic law. This Tehran–Damascus axis has long been important in Middle Eastern terrorism and has served as the most potent source of state sponsorship. Iran and Syria not only lend political credibility to foreign terrorists; they also provide logistical support that includes money, false documents, and arms. This is illegal under a United Nations treaty in force since 2002, the International Convention for the Suppression of the Financing of Terrorism. Worse, the two states train many Sunni and Shia terrorists in black arts. On hidden training grounds, in barracks, and in classrooms unseen by much of the world, staffed with specialists in guerrilla war, bomb-making, surveillance, computers and electronics, and the like, trainees delve into their crafts. Such hands-on training is overseen by some of the world's experts, such as the Revolutionary Guards, whose veterans' list begins with Mahmoud Ahmadinejad, the hate-spouting man who until mid-2013 was president of Iran. The Iranian–Syrian effort is nearly as dangerous to the world as the Soviet bloc training of terrorists in the 1970s and 1980s because it is every bit as calculated, well funded, protracted, and officially protected.

Despite three decades of such training of terrorists and giving them weapons, Iran had never felt the sharp cut of strong sanctions by the international community. And it has been a problem to which Washington turns only occasionally, as in June 2011 when the Obama administration placed limited sanctions on several Iranian groups, including the Revolutionary Guards. These and other economic tools are being strengthened now to good effect. Global coordination of our partners on such efforts must be a priority, especially given Iran's successful drive toward development of nuclear bombs—at the very time some European states are abandoning plans for peaceable civilian use of nuclear energy. Iran already possesses much more than is needed for a "radiological dispersion device"—which could be used by Tehran or given covertly to a terrorist ally. Varied overt actions to contain Iranian aggression are appropriate for the international community and NATO, and to other organizations, while the United States may consider covert actions of its own or via allies. One remembers that Turkey stopped tolerating the illegal absurdity of Syrian training grounds for Kurdish terrorists in about 1998 and forced Syria to eject the Kurdistan Workers' Party. War was not required, although force was threatened. When can NATO do the same with Iran and its deadly terrorist assets?

"Virtual sanctuaries" in cyber space are a problem well appreciated by the White House authors of the 2006 and 2011 national strategies against terrorism. The National Security Council's Richard Clarke did pioneering work on the problem for Democratic and Republican administrations. Terrorists use the Internet for communicating, staying abreast of political news, conducting detailed research, performing reconnaissance, and even training online. Weapons manuals are circulated, from published Western army handbooks to the newer "jihadi encyclopedia" formats with sections on small arms assassinations, "killing with cold steel," and making poisons. Names of useful contacts for getting into remote areas may be hidden in code if both parties are sophisticated. Instruction on hidden banking, such as the nearly paperless *hawala* system,[7] may be found. Computer-hacking instruction and information on computer code is available, some of it specifically aimed at fellow jihadis. And terrorist *fatwas* are published to point out prospective targets. Thus Californian émigré and Al Qaeda propagandist Adam Gadahn (now one of the FBI's "Most Wanted") signed onto the web in May 2011 exhorting Islamist Americans to visit gun shows and buy automatics, allegedly easy to obtain without background check or ID card.[8] Such things have appeared in print before: *The Anarchist's Cookbook* or Che Guevara's manual *On Guerrilla Warfare* might be bought in a shop or ordered through a "Liberation Books" sort of catalogue.

Such resources are now easily accessible—and printable—with no need for checkbook or credit card, and no need to take the risk of physically appearing in a suspicious store or a library. Virtual training will never match the actual physical sites in utility and results, but it may work. The colorful Al Qaeda magazine *INSPIRE* is the latest in such practical instruction and encouragement. If someone wanted to know "How to Make a Bomb in the Kitchen of Your Mom," *INSPIRE* gave instruction in the first issue (July 2010). Ten further editions appeared on the Internet by mid-2013.

To block the most dangerous of these efforts, there should be limited, very selective policing of the Internet. Did not every cattle town of the early 19th-century West need a sheriff? Do not most new frontiers see cases of savage killings and unrestrained crime until limited policing appears?[9] A student of civilization's frontiers in the 5th century B.C., Athenian historian Thucydides knew that without hard work in the world's seas by legitimate navies, piracy will prevail at the expense of the commerce of normal people. We are relearning the lesson today, and states are deploying naval patrols accordingly, as in the Horn of Africa, with excellent effect. Cyber war can now do far more economic damage than many older terrorist bombings. Strategies of economic warfare are self-consciously practiced by Al Qaeda, by Marxist-Leninists, by state parties in China and Russia, and by the West's own eco-terrorists, among others. Therefore, the time has come to take down or alter certain websites of violent groups. Skilled experts under careful oversight should be deleting one or two bits of information in the bomb recipes, or warping the instructions by adding a measure of a chemical that will neutralize the planned chemical reactions. There may also be need of a strategy for limited policing of incitation and hate speech by terrorists on the web.[10] This has only been whispered about; public officials owe us a more open discussion.

Our principles of liberty and our distaste for regulation steer many citizens away from even so limited an effort as having a "sheriff" for virtual frontier lands. Yet we know precedents in U.S. law and the law of other democratic states. One of the FBI's most well-accepted programs is policing web solicitation for child pornography. Several U.S. states debated and passed "hate speech" laws that single out inflammatory talk of certain kinds as illegal and punishable. Such laws did not exist before. Why would a citizen be more willing to allow access to a bomb-making instruction video than he would a right-winger "shouting" in capital letters on the web about homosexuals? Does not the present need for occasionally intervening against "incitement" harken back to one of the oldest of American principles—that the right to free speech is for sane political discourse and does not include any right to shout "fire" in a crowded theater? British law is as vigilant as our own in protecting political discourse from multiple perspectives and parties, and hot rhetorical jabs in parliament are world renowned. But the U.K., even under a Labour Party government, found that certain alien mullahs require deportation because they stop at nothing in inciting certain Muslims to violence in the United Kingdom. On occasion, London has even raided a mosque. France has a program for licensing imams who hold the venerable positions of teachers and leaders in mainstream Islam. France thus precludes some public access to political hot bloods, foreign agents, or violent ignoramuses, while promoting learning and worship in accord with traditional study of the Koran.[11] Saudi Arabia, where much of the modern problem began, has turned to "de-radicalization" programs and also to supervising the web. Limited policing of websites is a natural dimension of this kind of effort.

As every citizen knows, this is an important choice. Some experts counsel against any website censorship, arguing that on grounds of intelligence needs we must monitor them to learn about the terrorists. But security entities do so now and still can. Occasional intervention and limited policing does not mean we stop surveillance of "jihadi" postings or study of the radicals' online writings. But in unusual cases, U.S. authorities should decide to act—not merely observe. Our intelligence experts may also join in and become informants, or false friends, to the terrorists—a tactic of inquiry that has also worked in some on-the-ground policing of subversives in the open society.[12]

Another objection to doing anything about the violent political websites is that "Terrorists are so flexible they will reappear immediately on a site elsewhere." So, let them. Is the trained U.S. expert going to be so mentally slow that he or she cannot find the new website? And if authorities cannot find the new site, how likely is it that aspiring "jihadis" can find it? There are, as well, the small cadre of skilled *anti*terrorist freelancers now in this business (such as the SITE Institute) who point out hostile website lists and help police to track the web for particular Al Qaeda propagandists. These pro-democracy activists and "hacktivists" will not disappear. This objection about the sites reappearing elsewhere is evidence of a quitting attitude. It is the same as saying that the citizens' block watch committee, or the local beat cop, should ignore a notorious pick-pocket or heroin dealer because "If you arrest him, he'll get out and just go to work on a different corner." Modern terrorism does more damage than the picking of pockets. The Internet frontier really does need a sheriff or two.

## Diminish Underlying Conditions of Terrorist Support

No challenge in contemporary counterterrorism has been more discussed but less met than diminishing the support of terrorism. "The roots of terrorism," as many call them, are varied and complex and not easily dealt with by policy and strategy—especially at a distance from Washington. It has proven easy to call for "dealing with the roots of terrorism" but very hard to do so.

Terrorism explodes out of politics. In some foreign countries where terrorists are hidden, harbored, or trained, voting does not exist or is marred by the power-hungry, poor processes, or semi-anarchy, and a most vital need is to secure or recover the process of free and secret balloting. President Obama's counterterrorism strategy calls for creating "responsive government" in such places. That ideal is virtuous and may be effective. A fine old example is how the United States worked with the Republic of the Philippines against the Huk insurgency in the early 1950s. Defense Secretary turned president Ramon Magsaysay created confidence in elections and a system to secure them, called NAMFREL (National Citizens' Movement for Free Elections), which still works today. Citizens' observation teams ensuring the credibility and safety of voting booths and vote-counting centers made balloting popular where it had been untrusted. Magsaysay's innovations of political, economic, and military kinds (and steady counsel from American intelligence officer Edward Lansdale) turned the Philippines around.[13] Democracy came to be seen by Filipinos as truly practical rather than some questionable import from abroad. Today, the U.S. Marines and other officer corps examine this case study in their professional graduate schools, seeking out what limited lessons it offers to today's counterinsurgents in Afghanistan and Iraq.

In other places, the crying need may be for political initiatives flanked with economic aid. Consider U.S. foreign assistance. On a *per capita* basis, we give less than Japan or Germany or many other industrialized powers. On the other hand, most terrorism has little to do with poverty. In the case of the Huks, the Filipino and American governments had almost no money for economic aid, nor was it key to the success. Innumerable terrorists of today are well heeled and thrive in developed countries. On the other hand, millions of poor Asians and Africans face poverty while working hard for a better status without ever considering taking refuge in a terrorist group. For every Hezbollah administrator or guerrilla scoring propaganda points in Lebanon's slums handing out (Iranian-supplied) money and food to the poor, a half-dozen of their countrymen, just as poor, are too proud to ever join these Shia gunmen with their embarrassing allegiance to Tehran. But post-emergency relief by a joint U.S. military mission to "Provide Comfort" to Kurds doubtless kept many from listening to anti-American propaganda, and perhaps deterred some extremists from becoming armed militants at war with our NATO ally Turkey. And long-term engagement with anti-poverty programs in other places— such as Afghanistan and Iraq where we made war—would be a worthy and prudent form of foreign policy and public diplomacy.

One very effective weapon against terrorists is neither as mechanical as polling nor as material as food assistance. It is ideas, to counter terrorist ideology. For men like Dr. Ayman al Zawahiri, it is his ideological leadership that is his prime power. To deal with an enemy ideology we must think in non-mechanical, non-economic, non-military ways, considering schooling (theirs and ours), public diplomacy, and the way in which Washington acts on the world stage. The greatest American deficit in contemporary counterterrorist work is our failed performance in "the war of ideas." We are disarmed, out of ideas. While the cheapest of all arms are the weapons of the mind, we have few to none, and no plans for procuring or deploying more. Painful proof of this is the 2011 White House counterterrorism strategy, which has many exhortations to perform in this arena but virtually no new ideas for such a performance. The federal government worries over budgets for its international broadcasting media, but actually the problem is that government does not know what to *say* through existing media.

Why are we failing at this? According to scholars at Washington, D.C.'s Institute of World Politics, the United States lacks the essentials for this side of the contest with our enemies. Americans lack the *instinct* for political warfare—which is good for us at home but debilitating for our counterterrorism fights abroad. We have no *culture* in our Department of State or elsewhere that develops expertise in public diplomacy or measures effective use of it. We pay little attention to policy and strategy in public diplomacy. And when we do conduct public diplomacy it is inadequately coordinated with the other machinery of U.S. foreign policy. Until January 2013 the United States even bound itself by a 1948 law called the Smith Mundt Act that blocked officially made U.S. information programs from being available in the United States. For example, good Somali-language news programs made by the Voice of America for beaming into overseas Somali radio sets could not be monitored or enjoyed by Somali residents in American communities or by other Americans interested in Somali culture. So while U.S. public diplomacy hobbled itself, the Federal Bureau of Investigation was fretting over the fact that 30 Somali American young men had disappeared overseas to fight in Africa in what they name "jihad."[14] We all recognize how many other large immigrant communities in America still function in their native languages, more than English, but we will not permit them to see a U.S. government-produced program. This is wrong, and now that the law is rescinded, the best of such programming should be made available with simple and clear markers in multiple places showing that it is of U.S. government making.

While American taxpayers spend some U.S.$800 million a year on public diplomacy,[15] at home they never see its fruits, or get to make judgments about its quality and its worthiness for "export" abroad. Even American writers considering the meaning of occasional drops in favorability ratings of groups such as Al Qaeda tend to attribute the decline to public alienation by the bloodiness of the terrorists' acts—not good things the United States has said or done. America launched "Al Hurra" television for Arabic-speakers but reduced many foreign-language broadcasts in other tongues, many of which are important to anti-terrorism. The United States Information Agency was self-consciously broken apart in 1999. The federal government then ventured to open new offices, only to end up closing those in confusion later. The Office of Strategic Influence in the Rumsfeld Pentagon barely lasted a few months. A new post of deputy assistant secretary of defense for support to public diplomacy was scrapped by the incoming Obama administration. Meanwhile, the last decade has seen one senior State Department head of public diplomacy after another depart office, after short or indifferent service, usually returning to private life. The new *National Strategy for Counterterrorism* does not even dare to use the words "public diplomacy," let alone address the failure to influence foreign publics.

What is the answer? It may or may not include a new federal office created, staffed, and funded in full recognition of the significance of public diplomacy and its good prospects in an age of social media. But the real answer is free. We need to research, create, and otherwise fashion new arguments, and make them abroad with imagination and energy and force, accounting for the particulars of the audiences and their cultures. All the great skills of our trained diplomats must be matched by younger and better-trained diplomats who speak past their counterparts in foreign governments to address the man and woman in the street, and the youth: existing programs do focus on youth, and that is a good investment. But what we need are skillful arguments, more than a redoubling of technical channels or yet another TV station. In fact, radio is in many ways a more calm and thoughtful medium for serious discussion, and cheaper, when compared to television.

Advancing under the banner that "ideas matter," the United Statesshould wage both defensive and offensive campaigns. These need not be uniform; in the world of politics there is very limited value to "all of us singing from the same sheet of music." The messages should not be predictable. The more foreign voices the better. But while this defense is for an international audience, it can draw heavily upon universal principles: the dedication to character that a free society requires; the way in which government's authority is based upon the people's consent; the need for structural decentralization of power under a constitution; the care taken to protect political and religious minorities despite "majority rule"; the need for an independent and lively press; and peaceful, free elections which transfer power from one group to another in an orderly, bloodless way. Typical terrorist ideologues, be they Revolutionary Armed Forces (FARC) Colombians, New People's Army (NPA) Filipinos, or Africans in Al Qaeda in the Islamic Maghreb, want none of these things and usually oppose all of them. If Colombians and Filipinos and Tunisians can choose, they will usually choose well. U.S. public diplomacy must be built upon a defense of democratic politics and civil discourse as alternatives to violence.

But we need an offensive, as well. Existing programs show near-total neglect of healthy offensive spiritedness. It does no harm to assure Muslims, time after time after time, that our counterterrorist war is not with them but with the fringe that attacked us ... but it also does little good, when repeated year upon year. It would be better to combine such defense with an occasional sharp critique of the "jihadi" fever. Consider the penchant some of these extremists have for internal Muslim religious war. The world watched a Jordanian Sunni, Al Qaeda terrorist Abu Mussab al Zarqawi, open such a gulf by attacks on Shias. The gulf is implicit in Islam—between the mainstream Sunni faith and the minority Shia faith—but he ripped all veils away. Today we see that inherent divide in the numerous Sunni extremist attacks on Shia pilgrims and mosques. Instead of cowering from this subject, we might well ask aloud about the dangers of religious war posed by the quarrels of these competing Islamist ideologues. To take another

example, why do non-clerics such as Al Zawahiri and bin Laden pre-
sume to issue a *fatwa*? Or, why is it that so many terrorists (such as
Iraq's Zarqawi, Chicago's Jose Padilla, and the Lackawanna Yemeni-
Americans) have sordid personal backgrounds in petty crime? U.S.
spokesmen almost never broadcast this, and independent media do not
bother to help. Rather than lamenting the relative lack of speeches by
"good Muslims,"[16] we could do more to await the fine words—which
do, in fact, appear—and put them front and center in the debate.
When did the White House press spokesman last announce with fan-
fare one of the devastating critiques of terrorism published by a moderate and respected group of Muslim clerics? These appear often, as did
the New Mardin Declaration from a conference in Turkey in 2010.
Such healthy documents are created, yet our public officials say nothing to give them an appropriate reception. Middle East affairs expert
James Phillips has said that our greatest need in the counterterrorist
campaign is finding friends in the region—but instead of promoting
them we are ignoring them.

When another good document of this type appears, the president,
vice president, or secretary of state should open a press conference or
deliver a speech *leading* with the new declaration and discussing its
significance as a contribution to sanity in politics. Today there is no
such effort even in reduced form at the White House press spokesman's pulpit. Yet from there could come a vigorous announcement,
melded modestly into a half-dozen other news leads of the day. This
silence thus far from articulate and outspoken officials shows that our
government is not seriously engaged in public diplomacy. Performance
does not approach the stated policy. Imagination, spirit, and high-
mindedness will yield many good arguments, and those rather than
more office space or expensive senior executive service managers are
the beginning of an answer to terrorists and other violent extremists.

Lost upon Washington, after the Cold War receded into the rear-
view mirror, is the terrific power of the idea. Within U.S. government
we once had a better appreciation for the strength and grace of the
well-spoken word and the true political concept. During the Cold
War, the United States Information Agency articulated these through
radio waves, over many hundreds of miles and mine fields. Famed
Soviet dissident Alexander Solzhenitsyn declared that we in the West
have little concept of the power of the information that flew, free and

true, over the Iron Curtain. Lech Walesa, leader of the Polish resistance to Soviet rule, agreed when he paid compliments to U.S. official news organizations after Poland's emergence from communism. Yet most Americans forget our material support to Solidarity and its stirring Polish-language newspaper in the years when it mattered.[17] When the Czechs emerged from their status as political subjects, their dissident hero and president Vaclav Havel came to the Washington offices of Voice of America to thank its intrepid staff for their strategic and decisive role, and for being illuminating during long, dark years.

## Support Civics Education for a Fuller Understanding of Democracy

Specialists in civics and political science know that most American young adults are short-changed at school. This has been a steady concern of The Heritage Foundation[18] in Washington, D.C., but it is now also a concern at the *Washington Post*, where editorials of June 2011 and February 2013[19] have called for making civics "a national priority again." The conservative think tank and the liberal national newspaper make a notable match-up in a capital fractured by partisan politics.

Unless students are lucky enough to have a gifted teacher, or attend an unusual school, few graduate from high school understanding the foundations of free government. These include the concepts of inborn or natural rights to liberty, representative government through elections, and the logic and reasonability of natural law—which the Founding Fathers took to be a guide. Decentralization of government can be wisely done through federalism and separation of powers. There is much in the relationships, balance, and brilliance of that little phrase "law and order."[20] And in an age when our legal system is being probed by advocates of Koran-based *sharia* law, it is important that our youngsters learn why the Founders, most of whom were religious, refused to have an official state religion. Americans, going back eight and nine full generations, understood these things or were taught them; today our young adults vote without being well schooled in civics. Students are exhorted to be patriotic, but that is different from understanding *why* ours is a great country. Students are, by and large, taught to think that economics are more important than ideas and ideals, and that teaching does them wrong.

Civics teachers can do much more to show the genius of this governmental system. "Genius" is a carefully chosen noun, and no overstatement. Dr. Matthew Spalding observes that our founders in the 18th century created a constitution proving to be "the longest lasting, most successful, most enviable, and most imitated constitution man has ever known."[21] Since democracy was invented in ancient Greece, it has been practiced in myriad other places, and has sometimes failed. So the essential truths built into the American founding are, indeed, remarkable, if not always clearly understood. A better understanding of our political principles will greatly help our anemic "public diplomacy" while at the same time improving civics education at home. With enhanced understanding of political principles, our voters will better sort through the difficult questions that terrorism presents. Four concrete examples from today's debates over our response to terrorism illustrate the importance of these ideas.

First, what is legitimate violence? Terrorism may be properly condemned on principle as the enemy of sane governance. Yet, relativists and skeptics claim "terrorism" is just "violence we don't like." Distinctions are reasonable and appropriate: *terrorism is the deliberate abuse of civilians and non-combatants for political purposes.* But guerrilla war tactics by armed forces may be legitimate. Insurgency may appropriately and morally target the security forces of a government that is tyrannical. Our American Revolution is a model of that fact—standing in contrast to the blood-purges and dictatorship that adulterated the French Revolution after 1793. It was debatable whether the U.S. should be engaged in war in Syria in 2013; but there should be *no* debate over whether Syrian citizens have a right to oppose the Bashar al Assad regime without being called "terrorists." Observers of the fighting have noted war crimes on each side—which deserve punishment—but being in power for years has conveyed on the despot no God-given right to rule, and rebel attacks on his security forces are separable from terrorism, which is "the deliberate and systematic murder, maiming, and menacing of the innocent to inspire fear for political ends."[22]

Second, what is our State Department policy on violent groups that do use terrorism but also garner votes in elections? In past years this arose when European terrorists such as the IRA "Provos" and ETA Basques used political front groups which openly competed in elections (Sinn Fein and Herri Batasuna). Today some terrorists are so politically self-assured they compete openly as Hamas did in Palestine in 2006, and as Hezbollah did in Lebanon in the 2011 elections. U.S. policy, under Democratic and Republican parties, has been fairly consistent. Washington does not think it is enough that a group is merely popular. To be a legitimate political party with which the United States will formally engage, a group should at minimum take a principled stand against violence against civilians and be officially committed to reasonable politics, including civil discourse and respect for minority rights. This arose again as we examined the Muslim Brotherhood's political strength in Egypt during the Arab Spring.

Successful terrorist groups usually follow up their emergence into full state power by purging their opposition. Algeria's National Liberation Front (FLN) did so in 1962, killing thousands of countrymen and driving Algerians overseas by the hundreds of thousands. The Taliban, for its part, did ugly work in the late 1990s when consolidating power in Afghanistan. Hamas followed up its January 2006 electoral success in Gaza with gun battles in the streets and government building corridors against its Fatah opponents. If ferocity against political opponents and civilians has been a consistent strategy, almost no group that succeeded with it would give it up after victory.

Third, a question arises here at home as we manage the legislative and judicial side of counterterrorism. Why should non-citizens be granted privileges held by American citizens? Surely basic human rights are due to anyone anywhere, especially in America. But our court procedures need not deal the same with an immigration violator, an alien terrorist, and a *bona fide* citizen who is part of our "political compact" and fully invested in the future of America. There was an "Alien Terrorist Removal Court" in the federal system, created under the Clinton presidency and deserving of use in a limited set of cases, but never once used to this day. There is no threat to citizens' civil liberties if such a court does not use juries to try alien defendants, or uses evidence whose sources cannot become public as they would be in normal trials. Instead of treating alien residents and/or immigration law-breakers differently than U.S. citizens, Americans shy away from any such distinctions, hardly daring to mention them in polite company. But it is our principles which are universal, not our Republic. Full citizenship here has greater responsibilities, and it deserves greater rights as well.

There is an instructive fourth example of why the fight with terrorism demands a principled political understanding ... not just Special Forces. Why do some of our media report with near indifference (which they call "objectivity") on foreign terrorists' assaults on Americans? Everyone—especially journalists—know of this paradox. Yet many learned people, including journalists, insist upon ridiculing moral "labels" and put the word *terrorist* in quotation marks or avoid it entirely—even when the group itself embraces the term.[23] This is sometimes the published policy at major media organizations, and the set view of many reporters. After decades of studying the coverage of terrorism in democratic countries' newspapers, I believe that most reporters see themselves as rigorous professionals first and secondly as "citizens of the world." Being citizens of their own democracy often comes third. Legally and politically, there are no "citizens of the world"; that is merely a sentiment. Reporters covering something as serious as political violence should remind themselves on occasion that they are citizens of a land under terrorist attack. Winston Churchill, by blood half-American (and at times a professional journalist himself), observed, "I decline utterly to be impartial as between the fire brigade and the fire." His view of 1926 remains a healthy guide to the aspiring journalists now preparing themselves in our schools. Media outlets should all have printed codes of responsibility for covering terrorism—as some do—and perhaps Churchill's words deserve a place within them.

That fourth and final example from today's public discourse deals narrowly with reporters, who have every right to challenge it. But the point brings us back to the understanding of terrorism vis-à-vis modern democracy. Some past national security strategy documents have argued that democracy is the best antidote to terror. That must be qualified. Many democracies have at times been plagued by terrorists. Italy was almost paralyzed in the early 1970s, and Sri Lanka was bloodily divided by the Liberation Tigers of Tamil Eelam (LTTE) for decades until May 2009. Other democracies have been so bedeviled by attacks over time as to be dragged into acceptance of martial law, as were Uruguay and Turkey. The very openness of democracy allows violent ideologies to develop. The democratic system is not quick to recognize, let alone counter, such new threats, which is why Japan saw but did little about the rising face of Aum Shinrikyo.

So, what do analysts mean when praising democracy as a solution to terrorist problems? Liberal democracy creates openings for healthy new ideas and the working out of grievances and the satisfaction of the need for change. New parties may rise or fall. Would-be dictators may be examined by the media and rejected by voters, while moderate but talented people sometimes prove successful in public life and serve many terms as legislators. In dealing with the Sikh minority early in the 1980s, India opened up political space and gave concessions as well as deployed security forces, and thus New Delhi drained away the militancy. Our own Founders envisaged an "extended republic" built on liberal democratic grounds. A dozen civil wars are avoided in every decade of modern world history by the genius of representative and flexible government. This system can "drain away discontents," and channel activism and new voices into open political forums, and thus literally prevent the creation of terrorist groups. When hardened ideologues *do* forge a terrorist group, as is inevitable in so large and diverse a populace as the modern democratic republic, many would-be recruits will see too many alternative and healthier paths and thus disdain the terrorists.

When our civics classes deal with terrorism, they should reveal the ways in which democracy challenges terrorists and absorbs the more rational among them; in many countries, a few reformed terrorists even emerge in government or the universities. To put the problem differently: experts say that the major challenge posed by Al Qaeda today is its prompting of "self-radicalization" among citizens of democracies. That is half right. We already are avoiding radicalization, of millions, by openness, liberality, sobriety, and maintaining healthy political institutions. It is only a tiny minority who are at risk of self-radicalizing or taking prompts from a foreign power such as Al Qaeda.

So, too, can advancing democracy overseas tend by degrees toward undermining terrorism. In appropriate ways, our foreign policy should encourage the growth of responsible, limited free government, for these reasons and for our own interests. Democratic nations make the best partners, and historians agree that they are far less inclined to war than despotisms. So the very character of this democratic system of government is a natural advantage in maintaining our security. How can it be maximized?

Actually, the "export" or promotion of democracy has a part in every single national security strategy document published by every single White House during all recent decades.[24] More or less emphasis upon the point is natural; the level of interest rises and falls, depending on the president and his party. But the principle melds idealism and American self-interest, and it is always there in our official strategy papers. The means of realizing this dimension of grand strategy include presidential orations, his visits to foreign capitals, our official media such as Radio Marti beaming into Cuba, appropriated dollars going to overseas projects such as those of the Free Trade Union Institute, public construction projects in war zones such as Afghanistan or Iraq, aid to third world zones ravaged by nature, and even the proper deportment of our men and women in uniform who represent us overseas. In these and dozens of other ways we try to "advertise" our form of government and suggest its applicability abroad.

Among the more successful institutions that carry on this work is the National Endowment for Democracy. This privately managed, board-directed entity was created in the Ronald Reagan administration. Quietly, and with a budget provided by a mix of tax dollars and private donations, the endowment works abroad to promote the creation of new political parties, trade union newspapers, and the like. In one post-Soviet challenge, the country of Moldova, the National Endowment for Democracy (NED) gave U.S.$47,000 to an Association for Participatory Democracy, $184,000 for a Center for International Private Enterprise, $44,000 to a pair of centers encouraging independent journalism, and $18,000 to a National Institute for Women of Moldova. This encouragement of democracy's roots is what *we* can do abroad to deal with the truest "roots" of extremism and violence: teach and foster sane political alternatives.

Most Americans would not want to be tested on precisely where Moldova lies in Europe, and anyone can challenge such micro-grants on the grounds that American recipients at home (e.g., in Detroit) are more deserving of U.S. funds. But consider: the moment an international terrorist organization emerges from an obscure country (such as Moldova, Albania, Yemen) and attacks Americans, do our legislators not debate whether we might have assisted proper governance in this region and avoided the attack? Do congressmen not then turn to discussing aid programs, while senators sponsor bills to train the interior ministry's intelligence unit or the local police there? They do, and they would. The challenge in foreign policy is to look down the road to see where sage limited investment will (a) make friends abroad and (b) forestall larger security problems later. So the very obscurity of the Republic of Moldova (which, unlike Albania and Yemen, has not yet seen Al Qaeda) well illustrates why limited foreign aid is a good anti-terrorist tool. But that obscurity explains why, in years past, such politicians as Republican Hank Brown of Colorado and Democratic Party men Dale Bumpers of Arkansas, Senator Byron Dorgan of North Dakota, and Republican John Conyers of Michigan have often taken to the congressional floors to *oppose* money for the National Endowment for Democracy.[25]

Citizens of the United States should do the opposite. Kenya's chief justice was a former NED grantee. After violence in past elections, Kenya had better ones in 2013. Kyrgyzstan is a new republic fighting to find its democratic ways, avoid the extremists who lurk within and without, and stand up outside the shadow of the Soviets and Russians. Few know it, but the State Department created a press in the capital Bishkek which has been publishing pamphlets and books for a decade. Revolution in Egypt came as a surprise but there had been pro-democratic NED projects on electoral reform there in past years. These are the good fruits of well-placed seed monies. The 1,000 small grants that NED emplaces around the world each year are the work of a foreign policy Johnny Appleseed. There is room enough in our national budget for such small things; it would be worth forgoing procurement of a few tanks and aircraft. Ideas, too, are weapons. The single best candidate for focused new grants are private schools in countries such as Pakistan and Indonesia where, too often, religious madrassas are poisoning minds instead of enlightening them.

### Our Foreign Trainees Can Catch Al Qaeda Men Too ...

So quietly and calmly that almost none of our citizens know of it, federal agencies are meeting certain threats abroad before they hit us at home. The United States has over decades built a network of training academies and programs to create capacity for self-defense in our partner states and alliances. Partnering with Germany, our George C. Marshall European Center for Security Studies has graduated 1,400 women and men in counterterrorism studies. There are five academies run by the U.S. for foreign police, and there are graduate schools inside and outside Washington, D.C., teaching officials and other representatives from scores of countries. Other operations, as varied as these, are noted in the State Department's annuals called *Country Reports on Terrorism*.

Croatia, one of the Mediterranean region's newest NATO members, has made systematic efforts with U.S. technical assistance to fight terrorist financing, enhance cyber security, participate in exercises with U.S. troops, and contribute men and money to the anti-Taliban war in Afghanistan. Estonia has fighters alongside our own in the drug-dirty Helmand Province of Afghanistan, and is giving state monies to the overall anti-narcotics program. Meanwhile, with U.S. Defense Department counter-narcotics and counterterrorism funds, Estonia is improving its own border entry points at home. It is a leader in cyber security, with a revolutionary center for such work built for NATO, much to American advantage. Montenegro, a new republic within the abandoned borders of the old communist and terrorism-supporting state Yugoslavia,[26] is another partner, receiving U.S. training assistance for its Special Anti-Terrorism Unit within the police forces. Montenegro has prosecuted and convicted a large group of ethnic Albanian terrorists, including several U.S. citizens. The state also worked on creating a national counterterrorism strategy, improved its countering of terrorist financing, and aided the "coalition of the willing" in Afghanistan. One could go on listing our foreign trainees, but these few examples from Central Europe suggest how *our own* interests are served by these "foreign aid" programs.[27] Even small states can be a big help.

## Push for Public–Private Partnerships

Homeland security expert William Parrish notes that three-quarters of U.S. critical infrastructure is in private hands. This reality—widespread private property ownership—means that countering terrorist threats is a problem for corporations and smaller businesses, not just citizens, on the one hand, and government, on the other. And some of the most creative thinking and successful projects in security have been in the area of partnerships between business and government at its lower levels.

If one considers how a diminutive "city" such as Disneyland in Ana-heim, California, or the rebuilt World Trade Center in New York, is owned and operated, it is easy to recognize that millions of hours a year are devoted to security by private employees. Government's interest and involvement are inevitable, but most expenses and responsibilities are managed by corporations. This is even true of security forces at many of our nuclear power plants, where a worldwide commercial enterprise such as G4S Wackenhut has specialized in this area.[28] We have many threats to our nuclear plants, naturally, but there are also robust defenses and there have been no successful terrorist attacks on them to date. Another example of private-sector roles in nuclear security is the work of the nation-wide organization Business Executives for National Security, which has helped to organize the deactivation of thousands of nuclear warheads from old arsenals, reducing the risks of theft or sale for terrorist purposes.

The cyber world, one of the new frontiers of security studies, is another area for public–private partnerships. Internet carriers Verizon, AT&T, and Centurylink[29] are at work with our National Security Agency, the Defense Department (Cyber Command), and the Department of Homeland Security on technical means to scan digital traffic in the expectation of early trapping of malware and other malicious activity. The private sector is spending its own money to make this trial union possible, just as government is investing taxpayers' dollars. Privacy concerns blossomed in 2013 and these are inevitable. But every computer user has faced the drama of a virus or a denial of service from hacking or other criminal activity, and thus every computer user understands something of the threat terrorists could pose. Defense contractors—to take one example—have frequently been hacked. In mid-2011 a major company of this sort located in the Washington, D.C., area, and just then advertising special training courses in information technologies to the public, was humiliated by its own major systems being breached! So our U.S. defense program, just beginning but growing fast, deserves close scrutiny in Congress and the corporate world—not just for problems, but for the prospects it opens. Budget hawks looking for new places to cut defense spending should swoop past, not prey upon, these nascent governmental programs linked into public corporations.

Allies are also at work in public–private partnerships. Canada's first published national counterterrorism strategy (November 2012) emphasizes that dimension of security. Europe has held many international meetings of governments and consultants, especially since about 2006. British planners for the London Olympics of 2012 were connected to private partners, including the Control Risks Group. Germany developed a formal approach to bringing corporate experts into cooperation with government. In 2005 the German federal government published a *National Plan for Information Infrastructure Protection*, aimed at anticipating and reducing problems in information security. Three years later the Germans released a risk and crisis management strategy as well, outlining a structured approach that could work for companies and public offices alike. An attack on energy sources could lead to a cascading threat to society and industry at large, and the same is true in the cyber realm, so the Germans are at work to build protections and resilience into their national networks.

In short, national governments have always thought hard about their responsibilities for security; but increasingly, and intelligently, governments are thinking about these responsibilities as shared with the thousands of businesses that can help to reduce dangers to citizens and manage any crisis that does arise. American corporations can and must help. FedEx has taken an impressive leadership role in these efforts to partner with government,[30] and the recent attempt by Al Qaeda members in Yemen to bomb UPS cargo planes underscores the mutual interests. There is another way to examine the problem of terrorism which leads toward a very similar solution: those in the business world most worried about government regulation have an opportunity in these partnerships; by being forward-thinking and helpful, businessmen may help to shape what Washington does and help to control what regulations are to come from federal hands.

## Deepen Training of U.S. Intelligence Analysts

For all our efforts at building a global net to fight a global enemy, we must also improve our own analytical resources. In this past decade of war with Al Qaeda, thousands joined or were assigned to the ranks of our intelligence personnel. The Federal Bureau of Investigation has hired some impressive Ivy League graduates. The Bureau and the

Department of Homeland Security have brought on board hundreds of new people each year. But national needs do not rest there—and progress is undercut by departures, which take half-trained personnel and executives away before they are true governmental assets. If America were to have the opportunity to improve and enhance training, what main areas would deserve our first attentions?

First, "ideas have consequences." Analysts have the same challenge—at a different level—as other American citizens: understanding the bizarre and horrific ways in which terrorists think. "Psycho-logic" is what former CIA profiler Jerrold Post calls this. Terrorists are almost never insane persons; they are calculating political actors. They study, debate, and examine the approaches of past terror groups. By contrast, "non-terrorists" in democracies are too skeptical. Instead of understanding the communism of the FARC insurgents in Colombia, observers assert that they are not communists—merely drug-dealers. Ronald Reagan, no schoolmaster, understood ideas and their power at rich levels, and part of his success in the presidency was due to understanding communist ideology, knowing it must be contested, and believing it could be contained and outlasted. America needs such an approach today to ideologies as diverse as communism (FARC and ELN in Colombia) and neo-Nazism (a narrow but brutal part of life in the Czech Republic, Russia, and the United States, among other countries).

Islamism, so widespread as to be our country's largest security challenge of the day, can still fly under our radar screens even now, years after 9/11.[31] Outgoing Senators Susan M. Collins (Republican, Maine) and Joseph I. Lieberman (Independent, Connecticut) released a strong report on the lessons from the Fort Hood, Texas, shooting of November 2009. Calling it "the worst terrorist attack on U.S. soil since September 11, 2001," their Committee on Homeland Security and Governmental Affairs drew upon years of work in crafting the report,[32] and it came down hard on the failures of the Defense Department and the FBI to perceive the threat. The central failing was one of understanding—not firearms detection, not an individual's gate pass, nor U.S. national border controls, and not bad morale in our army. Our personnel failed through not understanding that Islamism, a violent ideology, is the enemy in the larger fight.

Army Major Nidal Malik Hasan did not just show a few "red flags" that intelligence officers should have spotted. He was a veritable circus barker, calling out, over and over again. In PowerPoint demonstrations at professional military schools, and when attending conferences, this psychiatrist made a show of his views on the Koran, its supposed support for killing, why suicide terrorism could be "understood," and on and on. Senators find it incredible that his supervisors and case investigators let him slide. One army boss even praised Hasan's passion for helping us all understand the global war on terrorism! Americans have always been skeptical about ideologies, making us prone to overlook terrorists who believe in them, terrorists who dream of making floors in Fort Hood run red with blood. Public defense came down to citizen-heroes such as Michael Grant Cahill and John Gaffaney, who literally attacked the shooter with chairs, and then Officer Kimberley Munley and Sergeant Mark Todd, whose bravery and guns ended the fight.[33] This is not one more example of random gun violence in America; it is the impact of the "war of ideas" which we have not taken seriously. Ideas have consequences. There will always be another "lone wolf terrorist," just as there will always be one more new conspiracy cell in a small town or big city. Our grand strategy must confront the ideas and confront the ideologists who are most often responsible for these new individual recruits. In an essay of 2010, a gifted authority on world religions wrote that we may think ideology is just a sideline problem, but in fact it is the essential problem in contemporary terrorism.[34]

Counterterrorism analysts take years to train; these are not "summer hires." The educational process demands layers of graduate education (above normal university levels), and thus it requires patience from us all, and a decent salary for the analyst, even though the professional seminars and higher schooling take hours away from the job. There must be immersion in the history of terrorism,[35] and the methods used by a given group under study, and terrorism's anti-historical, cross-geographical patterns of behavior, because very similar behaviors appear on many continents, almost without need of local context.[36]

Return for a moment to U.S. Army doctor Nidal Hasan at Fort Hood, and speculate. Imagine a smart young analyst, hired into the FBI after her three years of college training in classical Arabic language, and assigned before the murders to scrutinize Hasan's lectures and opinions. She sees that the subject of the inquiry is a medical man and thinks: "healing." A civilian, she sees an army officer, and thinks: "service and patriotism." She hears a tape of a Hasan talk at the Uniformed Services University of the Health Sciences in Maryland, a speech indulgent of Islamist militants; she could think: "bold, out of the box analysis." She hears more passion than appropriate in a doctor's voice, but checks herself, thinking: "I'm not Muslim, and on this issue they feel differently than I." Imagine this same young lady ten years later. Now she has taken the Defense Intelligence Agency's course for Advanced Terrorism Analysis and similar professional training. Loving the job, she carries in her mind another decade of professional reading. Assigned to this same case, what might she see? Now she knows that more than a few medical doctors have become terrorists, including Al Qaeda's Ayman al Zawahiri; a car-bomber at Glasgow Airport in 2007; the duo who led the Popular Front for the Liberation of Palestine, George Habash and Wadi Haddad;[37] and medical student Che Guevara.[38] Our analyst knows Major Hasan to be a psychiatrist, so she may recall Frantz Fanon, the French-trained psychiatrist who in the 1950s joined the Algerian National Liberation Front (FLN), treated their wounded, wrote books with cerebral defenses of terrorism, and penned propaganda for the underground's newspaper *El Moujahid*. And, while Hasan is a U.S. Army officer, our analyst has now seen many counterintelligence briefings, and knows how recent years have uncovered both military officers and civilians with top security clearances who are U.S. traitors, including John Walker of the U.S. Navy and Aldrich Ames of the CIA.

Of course, this analyst is a creation, and her mental pathway above is only speculative. But taking the brief intellectual journey with her gives a better sense of why we must have well-educated analysts—*not just more* analysts. According to a *Washington Post* study of July 2010, tens of thousands of people work in the Washington, D.C., area on some aspect of counterterrorism. Yet it is a safe bet that when they began to be paid, only a few hundred really understood terrorism, let alone its recent history.

A final recommendation for improving our analytical capabilities is technical rather than "human." If previously decision-makers were short of information, the 21st century buries citizens in information. There are databases of staggering capability. There are networks that yet further enhance what individual databases can achieve. There are mind-bending programs that can search through landfill-size data dumps and find the single clue, the missing telephone number, the obscure rural Malaysian address, or the ATM ticket that can break open the investigation. But none of this may be familiar to a federal contractor proud of his new security clearance or that smart person with collegiate Arabic language training. All of it is foreign to most graduating from universities in literature, history, urban-planning, or journalism. Many a smart soul can be posted to an intelligence "fusion cell" and dramatically underperform. The country requires good data managers and good training for the use of information at the analytical level. Not every American is up to that challenge.

### Keep An Eye On *All* Kinds of Violent Extremists in the United States

The challenges of intelligence and analysis relate to our next recommendation. As Al Qaeda's core membership has come under terrific pressures during the last decade, other problems have remained or may emerge in stronger forms, and we must not be blind to them. The August 2011 horror in Norway—mass shootings and a bombing by an anti-Muslim—is but one suggestion of caution for any who equate terrorism today with the Koran. The militant ideology of Islam*ism* is, indeed, the latest threat to America and the greatest at present, and even so, it is just one wave of terrorism among others. It was not Islamists who caused the FBI to create several dozen Joint Terrorism Task Forces in the 1980s. It was not Islamists who blew up the Alfred P. Murrah Federal Building in 1995. America has seen massive property damage, intimidation, and, in some cases, killing from many other kinds of fanatics. Anarchism, animal rights, neo-fascism, anti-federalism, and perversions of the Jewish and Christian religions[39] all bear watching on our home front—although surely we are "at war" with none of them.

Even "Greens" have their ghosts. Sabotage by extremists who are desperate to save lab animals, oppose the meat industry, or prove that "all life is created equal" began in one sense with the ugly little maiming devices built by Theodore Kaczynski, also known as the Unabomber. Today the FBI lists of terrorism incidents are dominated by his successors, who favor arson over explosives. Anarchists were fond of killing in this country a century ago; they largely fell quiet, but today the news from Western Europe brings out their ideology again. No one expects pro-Israel activists to bomb or discharge firearms in American streets now, but such actions came in the 1970s and early 1980s, usually against Soviet bloc targets, and are instructive to us as to how various may be the paths of terrorism. Take another New York City example: the eccentric cult Aum Shinrikyo had an office there. Its leader might have chosen to strike in New York, on the same April 1995 day, to support the cult's actions in Japan.

Americans cannot think that religion and politics mixed in an impossible way in Aum. Here at home citizens have endured episodes by the Phineas Priesthood, Aryan Nations, and the World Church of the Creator, all of which claim Christian faith yet spin off individuals who murder or maim. Small black Muslim communities belonging to Al Fuqra, an organization that in the distant past committed arson and murder, have been tracked on a web page of the Colorado State Police; these communities may remain in several U.S. states and Canada. Stewart Bell's book *Cold Terror* on Canadian security issues[40] publicizes the existence of Al Fuqra, which has sought to stay below the public and police radars. White adherents of the Ku Klux Klan (KKK) have also crisscrossed the U.S.–Canada border, and many cells are active to its south today. When their "fan base" here appears weak, they may seek racial fellowship abroad, in overseas countries where the population is Caucasian-heavy. In a 2010 working trip to Prague, the author told an interior ministry officer that former Louisiana politician David Duke (and past KKK member) had been lecturing in Russia and advertising his political outreach efforts on his website. My Czech interlocutor replied: "He was just here, too." The topic changed to Gary Rex Lauck, the Nebraskan known as "the Farm Belt Fuhrer," whose bulk printing and sale of neo-Nazi propaganda landed him for a time in jail in Denmark. "He was just here, too," said the official in Prague.

*The Turner Diaries*—the paperback manifesto for right-wing revolution in America which so intrigued Timothy McVeigh—contains most of what a citizen needs to understand why a federal building in Oklahoma City was destroyed, with 168 lives lost. That single book manifests how ideas have consequences and inspired half a dozen murderous plots by right-wingers. Propaganda for European neo-Nazis in recent years has sometimes been printed in the United States for shipment overseas—taking advantage of our easier laws. It is important for our analysts to understand these neo-fascist and militant right-wing political players, and to understand that many of them are revolutionaries—not merely hooligans. Hooligans and soccer thugs are more of a social problem than a political one.

Professional analysts owe it to their country to understand these fringe ideologies that have overtaken the hearts and minds of a few of their fellows. To do so, they need excellent published resources. It is not enough to have the engaging and fact-laden monthly issues of *The Intelligencer* from the Southern Poverty Law Center, because that is just one voice, not always authoritative. The FBI should return to printing its excellent *Terrorism in the United States* annual, which stopped after 2001; during these past few years it could have had more readers than ever before. There are other FBI products, but nothing so well focused on terrorist acts in the United States, and nothing in print so apt to lead a citizen to make an informed tip to authorities when he suspects terrorism is brewing.

Too little of good value has been released by the newer Department of Homeland Security (DHS). Thus far it has made use of intelligence produced at other agencies and little more. It has not met hopes for growing into a contributor to the intelligence community, though it is key to the process of creating multilayered U.S. government "fusion" cells (the efforts of which were slammed by a Senate report of mid-2012). Turnover in this department's senior positions has hobbled development of deep and sound work. When the DHS Office of Intelligence and Analysis produced an assessment in early April 2009, daring to address "Right-wing Extremism" in America, some conservatives attacked it. The DHS should have used that moment to publicize findings that justified the study. Instead, it neither defended nor dismissed its product, choosing to gut the little office that wrote the paper. Apart from a very few lines by Secretary Janet Napolitano a week after the issue date, the affair ended. Thus DHS missed an opportunity to do one of the things it was created to do: advise the U.S. public and its security professionals about domestic threats.

## Understand the Risks in "Talking to the Terrorists"

Established U.S. policy has been to refuse to negotiate with terrorist groups. Spies, diplomats, and other liaison officers might listen and even "talk," but it was most unusual for any American government to bargain or dangle concessions. There are only a few dollar pay offs on the published historical record and not many other kinds of official concessions to terrorists. Critics often say that this hardline, standoff-ish policy "demonizes" terrorists. But terrorists demonize themselves by their own horrid acts against the innocent. U.S. policy is firmly signaling what democracies can, and cannot, tolerate by way of politi-cal activism. U.S. officials have generally believed that nothing excuses terrorism. After many years, the United Nations finally agrees with them and formally declares as much.

But the issue of whether one should negotiate with terrorists arises with every hostage-taking. Most victims' families are naturally ready to pay, or make concessions, and they often do so through private inter-mediaries. Many hostage cases come with larger strategic problems to be dealt with by our State Department's senior diplomats. Presidents can find themselves drawn into the daily details of major hostage cri-ses. Jimmy Carter and Ronald Reagan are examples of earnest, well-intentioned chief executives who suffered resultant embarrassments, both involving messes in the Middle East. They learned anew why Henry Kissinger worked to keep President Richard Nixon clear of direct involvement in these painful and complex situations. There is no disputing the principle that the powers of the United States must be summoned to recover by honorable means any American held hostage. There is, however, a question of command and control. Generally, the work of crisis management settles at the level of the National Security Council, if necessary with the vice president chairing. If there is direct involvement by the president, this should be kept masked from the outer world, because the more he or she is seen to be absorbed by the crisis, the more the "value" of the hostages rises in their captors' eyes, and the more foreign enemies will later have an incentive to take other American hostages.

That is a question of practice. The wider question is one of prin-ciple, and it has become the single hottest topic in the field of terrorism studies, with the new literature usually urging talking to terrorists for pragmatic reasons. Is it appropriate to negotiate with violent extrem-ists? And if so, when? Some groups of recent years are led by horrific people, feverish for power, willing to use "any means necessary." Many terrorist groups are doctrinally committed, in writing, to repudiating "reformists," peace accords, and partition agreements. In such cases, opponents of terrorism charged with defending public safety find it difficult to accept this current intellectual fashion. U.S. citizens are better guided by an old Roman maxim, "War down the strong; bear up the weak." The Romans knew concessions are best offered after victory. When a democracy such as ours is attacked by organized terrorists—as opposed to pressured by advocates through peaceful democratic channels—there is a much higher likelihood that force will be required than that clever negotiators will get terrorists to yield.

Even where talks are theoretically possible, real opportunity may not ripen for years—during which resistance by the legitimate state may be required. And when talks are tried, they may fail. They often have in the Middle East. In Nepal, Communist revolutionaries walked out on peace talks in early 1996 and opened a bloody (and somewhat successful) war for power. In Sri Lanka, years of earnest Norwegian negotiations made no dent in the Marxist-Leninist or national separatist goals of the LTTE Tamil Tigers. An ideologically driven, well-led organization such as Al Qaeda today may well have to be beaten, or broken into pieces, before zealous, life-hardened leaders such as Ayman al Zawahiri would consider serious negotiations.[41] If he does, it would remain difficult to imagine him folding into the pacific political process—even if some of his rank and file might do so.

But other possibilities intrigue those in the security studies field. The Northern Ireland tragedy, which had seemed so endless, was not resolved by any crushing battle or pattern of defections, but in large part by multiparty negotiations and outside mediation. One suspects that even the pattern of factional attacks by scattered cells since 2008 has proven manageable, and that, overall, peace will hold. Might this be a model, for other conflict zones? All hope so. Some *think* so. But a sub-state force such as the IRA had comprehensible, geographically finite political objectives—not the unlimited policy ends of a transnational caliphate, the persecution of co-religionists, the eradication of Israel, etc. These possibilities enthuse a new school whose spokespersons include former ambassador Chester Crocker (among those successful in Southern African peace-making) and academics who study negotiations. Small institutions and activist think tanks that are optimistic about such negotiations include the Geneva-based Centre for Humanitarian Dialogue and our congressionally funded, privately managed U.S. Institute of Peace.[42] This question is practical for

Americans now, because it has leapt into the center of our Afghanistan policy considerations. Recall that for a decade starting in late 2001, U.S. policy in Afghanistan was simple and clear: help establish peace; open space for national elections (a historic first); and then encourage nascent democratic government. But in October 2010 it became apparent that the Obama administration was actively exploring negotiation options that could get the U.S. out, and get the Taliban in. Press reports said Americans were ferrying Taliban negotiators into secret locations for such talks. Can this negotiations strategy work? Despite some Americans' hopes, the answer is probably "No."

There are fewer mysteries here than usual for a government groping to understand a rising foreign actor. This is "Taliban the Second Time Around." We have eerie feelings of memory, as this entity fights to return to power. In October 1999 the United Nations, with U.S. approval, condemned this insurgency. Taliban was sheltering and training terrorists and allowing them to plan attacks. The UN reaffirmed at that time its conviction that suppression of such "international terrorism is essential for the maintenance of international peace and security." The Taliban had also drawn attention for its ferocious abuses of women and girls and its other human rights abuses, such as kidnapping of foreign diplomats (from Iran, ironically). At the time, New York Senator Hillary Clinton was among those harshly critical of the Taliban. By late 2010 Secretary of State Clinton had the United States involved in talks. What changed? A skeptic might say it is only policy that has changed, because now we are scheduled to leave most of Afghanistan. No one is pretending the Taliban has grown moderate. The best hope is that the Taliban may be distancing itself from Al Qaeda.

The Taliban's leader, the popular and credible cleric Mullah Omar, is the same leader the movement has had since its origins in 1994. Even if it bars any return by Al Qaeda to Afghanistan or otherwise changes foreign policies, the Taliban at home will be tyrannical in power—as it was when ruling most of the country in the late 1990s. The kind of "power-sharing" with other Afghan parties that negotiations experts hope for is most unlikely. In post-World War II Europe, Communists used "salami tactics" to slowly take over power in states such as Czechoslovakia and Poland, moving gradually one ministry at a time. Communists partnered with various front groups in Vietnam until sweeping all that away with violence in the final act of 1975. But to date, the Taliban has not even bothered to "partner" with any respectable political party it does not agree with. It thinks it is winning without doing so. Washington need not condemn Afghans who wish to engage in peace talks with the Taliban—Afghan politicians may feel compelled to do so. But the U.S. should take no role in this negotiations enterprise and not be a visible host of talks. Just because, ultimately, we may have to *accept* any terms the Ahmed Karzai government actually makes, it does not mean that the U.S. and NATO should publicly *approve* them. This process of negotiations is likely to end with the Taliban in power.

### Regain What Momentum We Had at the United Nations

It is as true as it is surprising: the United Nations has shown activism against terrorism. The progress is, in part, creditable to Kofi Annan's years as general secretary, not just the shock of 9/11. This limited momentum must now be perpetuated by Ban Ki-moon. The South Korean who is general secretary may wish another term, and if so Washington might be influential in agreeing upon agenda items for the near future.

As noted above, the UN headquarters in New York City implemented financial and travel sanctions against international terrorists in the 1990s. Beginning in the fall of 2001, the UN Security Council published resolutions condemning terrorist acts as a "threat to international peace and security." That language—whether for a diplomat or a lawyer—has but one meaning: the UN committed itself to action, not just anti-terrorist talk. So now we should hold the body to its commitment. We may insist that the UN's resolutions matter. We should advance U.S. initiatives in the UN and support other countries' best initiatives. Act as if positive action is expected of the UN. If momentum flags, or if the body takes actions adverse to American interests, Washington can and should threaten to reduce general support—political and financial. The Ronald Reagan administration used such a prod during the 1980s to limited but good effect.

Among the first actions required are against Iran, and they should be tough measures but short of war. Harsh sanctions on the government travel and banking sectors and others are appropriate. There should be as full a ban as possible on travel by any Revolutionary Guards—whose officers have appeared in such countries as Sudan and Lebanon to train Shia and Sunni terrorists and guerrillas. Iranian covert operations are even a danger now to Latin America. Regional allies—who have more to fear from Iran than we do in the U.S.—should provide further ideas that Washington can support.[43]

A second major question for the Security Council—and for Washington separately—is that of sanctioning Pakistan. The compounding evidence of long-term state support to Lashkar e Taiba, other Kashmiri militants, and the Taliban has become more than "disturbing." When to all this is added the overlooking of bin Laden's housing near a Pakistani army base, the sum of the evidence is shocking, given how friendly and regular had been our governmental relations with Islamabad. A major cut in U.S. assistance to the security sectors of Pakistan is the least that is appropriate; when the government protests, the honest U.S. answer will be, "Turn over more Al Qaeda and Taliban terrorists, and we may restore the aid next year." The U.S. should move closer to India (a major victim of international terrorism by Islamists) and expand economic and non-military cooperation. That would suit our other state interests as well, rebalancing a region in which Pakistan keeps a close alliance with expansive China.

### Push Creatively in Bilateral and Multilateral Ways

Most states are not supporters of terrorism; they are its victims. Based in lax regions, international terrorists attack and then vanish, returning only when it suits them. But as the early 20th-century fight against international anarchists proved, these lethal men and women are not spirits; they may be arrested. Governments have other useful options. The very fact that terrorism is so international means that the U.S. has a vast array of potential allies to be cultivated, coached, and supported. One of a score of examples is the "Sovereign Challenge" series on global security. In June 2013, the U.S. Special Operations Command led by Admiral William McRaven held discussions in Portsmouth, Virginia. Representatives came from 65 countries, including Afghanistan, Bahrain, Oman, Tunisia, and Turkey. Some states will follow a good U.S. lead in regional or international organizations, and a small coalition built there may often be more useful than unilateral action. Whether we want hard-nosed partners or just the "political cover" of a coalition, the UN can be useful to us.

Consider a typical and also critical counterterrorism issue: MAN-PADS, or man-portable air defense weapons systems. These missiles are more accurate and more powerful than the rocket-propelled grenade that destroyed a low-flying helicopter carrying two dozen Special Forces personnel in Afghanistan in early 2013. MANPADS have proliferated, and are made by countries that include Iran, North Korea, and Pakistan. These weapons already account for 800 civilian deaths in more than 40 attacks. MANPADS constitute a problem requiring prompt international action—now, before they are used to knock down an American airplane. If we do not install mechanical defenses on our big commercial passenger aircraft, we will rush to do so *after* the next catastrophe, while explaining away the deaths of 200 to 300 citizens on a passenger airliner. There are already one or two prototype programs, such as the American Airlines partnership with BAE Systems funded by the Department of Homeland Security in 2008. We should ramp up such work with other bidders and split the costs three ways: airline, government, consumers (via ticket prices).

But while this is a good and realistic plan for the U.S., it would only deal with several sides of a large problem. Al Qaeda and other sadists remain obsessed with dropping an airliner out of the skies. They can shift their focus to a foreign carrier coming into or out of the U.S.—such as a NATO country's state airways or charter flight full of tourists to the next Olympic Games. Recall how North Korea's government successfully deployed two agents to place a bomb aboard a South Korea-bound passenger liner in the run-up to the Seoul Olympics of 1988. Washington can work with great partners, such as the United Kingdom and the Republic of Korea; but what of all the other countries at risk? The U.S. Department of State has been given the inter-agency lead in ongoing efforts against MANPADS proliferation, worldwide. Under accords such as the Wassenaar Arrangement on Export Controls for Conventional Arms and Dual-Use Goods, our diplomats encourage foreign counterparts to recognize the risk and actively help with government controls. The Department of Defense supports the required negotiations and the Defense Threat Reduction Agency counsels missile-owning armed forces on secure storage. The Treasury Department seeks to block terrorist groups from purchasing these weapons.[44] And the FBI has "stung" and thus arrested prospective MANPADS black market purchasers, such as Victor Bout, a Russian caught in Thailand.

Americans often face such terrorism problems whose tentacles stretch into a dozen distant places, and this makes it apparent that effective action will be international action. The UN's International Civil Aviation Organization (ICAO) could help in controlling the production, transfer, and sale of MANPADS. The UN Security Council has already pointed to the terrorist threat from such missiles in a resolution of 2005.[45] It is now time, on this issue and certain others, to lead and push the UN to move from its condemnations of terrorism into the appropriate forms of international action required to block terrorist activities. If the world community lets this threat go, all will be ever responsible for the next success with terrorist MANPADS. Anyone who reads newspapers may see the obvious lessons of Mombasa, Kenya, where in November 2002, a pair of missiles fired by Al Qaeda zipped past a departing passenger charter jet owned by an Israeli company.

### Keep the Moral High Ground and Uphold the Law

The utility in leading and working with international organizations does, of course, have limits—we should not run ahead of common sense or of fundamental American national interests. Here are two topical examples—temptations from which we should stand clear. First, avoid the quagmire of "Protocol One"—a proposed change in international law that is popular but foolish. Second, stay far from the business of torture—a disaster in democratic counterterrorism. In both cases, the best policy is remarkably simple: deal with future challenges by proceeding as we did traditionally.

Protocol One is a 50-page document designed to expand, explain, and allegedly modernize the Geneva Treaties of 1949. Most countries ratified it; the U.S. and a handful of others have declined to do so. The issue arose in the 2008 political campaign; Senator Obama asked that we join other countries in ratifying the new document. The issue will arise again as international law extends its reach. But there is a problem with some of the proposed new language, which will undermine an international understanding of terrorism at the very time a common sense approach to countering it has developed so well. Key parts—especially Articles 43 and 44—will erode the Geneva conventions, like termites working into venerable pillars of custom and *laws of war that separate civilians from combatants.* This distinction is not just a foundation of decency; it is the essence of the difference between just war, on the one hand, and war crime, on the other.

For over a century, international law has required that belligerents adhere without fault to four pillars: obeying laws of war; bearing arms openly; wearing some sort of uniform; and keeping a chain of command (i.e., gunmen are responsible to legitimate authority). Terrorists spit upon these things that armies do faithfully, be they the army of Bolivia, the navy of Brazil, the air force of Argentina, or the coast guard of Chile. Terrorists take hostages and use civilians as shields, instead of protecting these innocents. Terrorists smuggle weapons secretly and kill with them in peaceable foreign cities before disappearing over a border. Terrorists are self-appointed, responsible to no one, or to some odd ideologist or charismatic leader, not a legitimate authority. Terrorists take pride in their shocking crimes, crimes that a true soldier reports up the chain of command as abhorrent and illegal. Terrorists issue press releases, claiming "credit" for these crimes. Why would modern international law change to obscure these distinctions? There is no good reason. The protocol claims it would "modernize" something that is valuable in part for its very age. The protocol would protect peoples struggling against "colonialist" and "alien" regimes and "racist" dominance, but this list is already out of date since the 1977 drafting, and it ignores horrendous other forms of despotism, such as communism and the Taliban's twisted *sharia* law, which it imposed upon the Muslims of Afghanistan in the 1990s. Sometimes, the most important new decision a statesman makes is to hold his old ground. The Protocol One issue is a case in which the new and jazzy offering is to be declined. Instead, we should remain protectors of Geneva law's four-part gold standard, while resisting the glister of this fashionable, new interpretation.

The second way we must protect international law and reason is continuing to punish torturers—rather than suggesting they are a new counterterrorist tool. There is no mystery about why, after 9/11, a few handfuls of detainees were abused. First, great dangers lingered out of our line of sight, making some Americans act in fear to secure the country at all costs. Would there be more airplane bombs? More anthrax? A nuclear weapon? Cyber attack on our banks? No one knew, but people were desperate to know. A few executives, government lawyers, and officers in positions of influence thus allowed forms of interrogation that had long been forbidden. Defending torture as a way to gain intelligence from terrorist suspects is studiously immoral.[46] But even if fears may trump intellects, the schoolmasters of history should rap their knuckles and make them pay attention to reality. Any student of French counterinsurgency in Algeria during 1954 to 1962 recognizes what the argument for torture means: it is a trap door ... the moral flooring falls away ... in the abyss awaits probable strategic defeat and certain moral failure. It did France no good to break the terrorist cells infesting Algiers—and break them France did—because the French public and the rest of the world were appalled by the techniques used and withdrew support for the war.[47] France lost.

Police training should emphasize the many and different methods that tradition and practice worldwide do allow. There is cleverness, deceit, persistence, use of other witnesses, personal appeals based upon research into the individual, legal, and acceptable forms of psychological pressure on the terrorist's friends or family, and on and on. Even in liberal democracies, outright lying to suspects may be legal to trick them into confessing what they have done. Stressful interrogations are legal too. Manipulation of a suspect's fears is commonplace, worldwide, in police work. What is not common in liberal democracies, and never should be, is torture—the infliction of extreme physical or mental pain, often leaving permanent effects, and designed to break down a subject, body and soul. It is illegal under American law and international law, and being at war (as we are with Al Qaeda and affiliates) cannot forgive it. No one can say what a given individual may do in the most extreme circumstances, but that has nothing to do with policy. When setting policy, including military and law enforcement standards, torture cannot be allowable.

Even if torture is occasionally successful at eliciting information, it is impractical. Why? First, experts think that even if nuggets of truth emerge from abusing suspects, so do pieces of fool's gold. Telling the two apart takes valuable time and wastes human and technical resources. Second, terrorists may prepare and study as surely as interrogators; they can lie and mislead. Terrorists may end up "talking" and give up enough truth to make their lies believable, only confusing the leads. A terrorist might tolerate great stress, as a strong man does in battle, and finally *appear* to give up to the interrogator a name ... the name of an innocent man or a rival terrorist. Such "hot information" would yield no useable intelligence. Third, the "ticking time bomb" scenario that fascinates TV viewers, and has a ringing defense from one or two public figures, fails as a reason for torture. Recall that the entire exercise of torture only gets its peculiar endorsement due to admitted ignorance—the need to know. So the problems of logic start with the fact that there may be no bomb. Or, there is a bomb, but the suspect under torture may not know that it was moved since he last saw it, or moved after comrades learned of his arrest. Perhaps there is a bomb but it fails for technical reasons, which is common. Terrorist conspirators can be wrong about whether there is any bomb—or a half-dozen bombs; compartmentalization of such intelligence is standard practice in the underground. These are among the very *practical* problems with an alleged "right to torture" based on a "ticking bomb." Nor should we forget a principle of political philosophy and ethics: one should set standards based on human norms, not freakish exceptions. And the first time a demented policeman defends his torture of a hated suspect with the "ticking time bomb" theory, when no explosion ensued, the responsible city police department would shrink back under bad conscience and public criticism, returning in unison to the saner, older protocols. What we should avoid for its immorality turns out to need avoidance on practical grounds as well.

These pages within Part III have not laid down a comprehensive plan for the wholesale remaking of our government's actions. We already have a series of strategy documents, published by successive White Houses. Our purpose here is to highlight places for change or enhancement—how we can do better. Creative minds in many federal agencies and our partner agencies overseas will doubtless make good suggestions as our joint efforts continue. The best of these may be found by a winnowing process and implemented. Terrorism is not going away. In fact, a few outspoken optimists need to be reminded that many veteran leaders of the Islamist terror movement are still in the field. Much remains to be done.

## Notes

1 Counterterrorism is usually less expensive and less personnel intensive than counterinsurgency. Unmanned aerial vehicles ("drones") are cheaper than fighter planes with their pilots and supporting infrastructure. Ideas for discrediting Al Qaeda ideology are free and can be crafted by diplomats already on salary, and passed through existing media and government-owned technologies. Some expenditures (e.g., paying police sufficiently or preparing against a bio-attack) equate to improvements in public health and safety preparations that should be made anyway and are thus not "extra." So, counterterrorism need not be overly expensive. War in just one place, Iraq, has been immensely more expensive than the worldwide but limited counterterrorist campaign now underway.

2 *New York Times*, June 5, 2011. Kashmiri, killed in mid-2011, was a leading suspect in the November 2008 Mumbai massacre and the May 2011 battle to take over Mehran naval base in Karachi. He belonged to the terrorist group Harkat ul Jehad e Islami.

3 Killed on September 30, 2011 were Anwar al Awlaki, once an imam in a Virginia mosque, and his American partner and co-editor Samir Khan. Untouched in the strike was Nasir al Wuhayshi, a former bin Laden bodyguard believed to command the Al Qaeda in the Arabian Peninsula organization enjoying success in Yemen.

4 Saif al Adel was Al Qaeda's security chief. From 2002 on he was in Iran for nine years and *may* now be in Waziristan (Pakistan).

5 The Taliban is moving away from Al Qaeda, favoring local affairs, according to my colleague Amin Tarzi, director of Middle East Studies at Marine Corps University.

6 Two important UN actions are the coming into law in 2002 of the International Convention for the Suppression of Terrorism Financing, and United Nations Security Council Resolution 1566 of October 2004; both carry working definitions of terrorism.

7 "Flying money," *hawala*, is an ancient and informal system of money transfer, based upon trust, from early days in China, the Indian subcontinent, and other regions—not just the Middle East. The system dwarfs the terrorist participants within it, but it is highly useful to terrorists.

8 Staff editorial of the *Washington Post*, June 7, 2011, which quotes Gadahn and adds that semi-automatics might be obtainable without papers at gun shows.

9 This "virtual frontier" metaphor comes via John J. Kane, a writer on cyber terrorism who drew the idea from originator John Perry Barlow, *Crime and Puzzlement: Desparados of the DataSphere* (San Francisco, CA: Electronic Frontier Foundation, 1990).

10 When a Kosovar Albanian named Arid Uka watched Internet videotape purportedly showing American soldiers raping a teenage Muslim girl, he was moved to shoot two U.S. airmen on a bus at Frankfurt airport. The posted video was fake, a scene from a commercial movie, not a real rape.

11 On Islamist expansion in Western Europe, see Lorenzo Vidino, *The New Muslim Brotherhood in the West* (New York: Columbia University Press, 2010).

12 These sentences are about the desirability of penetrating terrorist groups—not civil activist groups. Sometimes a government inquiry is required to determine the difference, but the difference is vital to freedom.

13 Major Lawrence M. Greenberg, *The Hukbalahap Insurrection: A Case Study of a Successful Anti-Insurgency Operation in the Philippines—1946–1955* (Washington, D.C.: U.S. Army Center of Military History, 1987). Intelligence and leadership were more vital than money or U.S. dominance. One recent article in a military journal deprecating this success, when studied, is likely to leave an analyst yet more convinced of the 1950s success, ironically.

14 Three Institute of World Politics (IWP) volumes of recent years about public diplomacy were by PhDs: Juliana Pilon, Michael Waller, and the institute's president John Lenczowski. The latter authored *Full Spectrum Diplomacy and Grand Strategy: Reforming the Structure and Culture of U.S. Foreign Policy* (Lanham, MD: Lexington Books, 2011). Most of my paragraph is from Lenczowski's pages and a March 2013 telephone interview with Pilon about the January 2013 change to the law—a change the IWP helped to bring about.

15 By comparison, the State Department requested US$1.6 billion to cover its security efforts in fiscal 2012, and the overall request (before possible congressional cuts) for the department and foreign aid both totaled US$59 billion, according to Walter Pincus (*Washington Post*, October 4, 2011).

16 Legitimate Muslim leaders could do more to condemn terrorism publicly, and they should, according to a mid-2011 poll of American Muslim citizens by Pew Research Center.

17 When I worked for the House of Representatives in the 1980s, Congress appropriated money for Solidarity and its newspaper; the funds were voted openly and then clandestinely delivered. Two decades later, in Warsaw, I was thrilled to be able to buy an aging, yellowing copy of this historic trade union newspaper that helped to erode the influence of communist totalitarianism.

18 The Washington think tank's valuable publications in this arena include Robert Reilly, *Ideas Matter: Restoring the Content of Public Diplomacy*, Special Report no. 64 (July 27, 2009).

19 The first was a *Post* staff editorial; the second was a guest editorial by Dr. Danielle Allen.

20 There are several comments that well express the challenges of protecting democracy in Bell's book *Cold Terror*. The Canadian notes that most voters in his country understand that "without national security, civil liberties are no more than theoretical." About the duty of government to keep citizens informed on "terrorists amongst us," Bell writes: "The public doesn't need calming. The public needs the truth."

21 "Introduction to the United States Constitution," in *The Founders' Almanac*, ed. Matthew Spalding (Washington, D.C.: The Heritage Foundation, 2001), 233, and a telephone interview with Dr. Spalding in July 2011.

22 I have cited this definition above, as well; it is from the Jonathan Institute, Israel, 1979.

23 Abdullah Azzam, for example, a Palestinian murdered in 1989, was a partner to Osama bin Laden. In a November 2001 videotape, bin Laden quoted Azzam as saying: "We are terrorists, and terrorism is our friend and compan-

ion. Let the West and East know that we are terrorists and that we are terrifying as well. We shall do our best in preparation to terrorize Allah's enemy and our own. Thus terrorism is an obligation in Allah's religion." Malise Ruthven, *A Fury for God: The Islamist Attack on America* (London: Granta, 2002), 209. Many such cases (in which "terrorists" accept that label) appear in the preface to my 2nd edition of *Terrorism Today*.

24 See, for past examples, George H. W. Bush on "The Contest of Ideas and the Nurturing of Democracy" in his March 1990 *National Security Strategy*, or William J. Clinton's many editions of such a document, including the sections on "Promoting Democracy and Human Rights" and "Emerging Democracies" in *A National Security Strategy for A New Century* (December 1999). Useful books on U.S. promotion of democracy were written by Gregory Fossedal and Joshua Muravchik during the 1980s.

25 In the latter 1980s, Representatives such as Jack Kemp and Jim Courter were among many who *did* support NED budgets and believed in fostering democracy abroad.

26 This lesser-known state sponsor indulged international terrorists who were Palestinians, as well as "Carlos," West European leftists, and, in at least one case, German right-wingers.

27 Our public diplomacy efforts may be undermined by misbehavior, or worse, by anyone the U.S. trains. Australia and the U.S. fund and supply Indonesia's "Ghost Birds," Densus 88, a special anti-terrorist unit, which has done well against Jemaah Islamiya (JI), including killing the mastermind of the 2002 and 2005 Bali bombings and other attacks that murdered Americans. But allegations of torture have touched that unit, and JI terrorist publicity material names the two foreign donor states in connections with these charges; Jamestown Foundation, *Terrorism Monitor*, vol. 9, issue 32 (August 12, 2011).

28 Since the 1960s Wackenhut has helped to secure some U.S. nuclear plants and sites overseas. The company has absorbed the Nuclear Security Services Corp. and is now part of a larger corporation with Danish and British capital called G4S.

29 *Washington Post*, June 17, 2011.

30 East–West Institute, "G8 Initiative for Public–Private Partnerships to Counter Terrorism," a discussion paper of November 2006.

31 Notably, commemoration materials about 9/11 sometimes focus not on the victims but on the dangers of public reaction against Muslims. After a decade, some newspapermen apparently still think the main problem in the U.S. is Americans' fear of Islam. The real problem for Americans, including Muslim citizens, is with Islamist terrorists.

32 *A Ticking Time Bomb: Counterterrorism Lessons from the U.S. Government's Failure to Prevent the Fort Hood Attack*, U.S. Senate Committee on Homeland Security and Governmental Affairs, February 3, 2011.

33 These are among the individuals later decorated by the army for heroism during the attack; *Washington Post*, May 24, 2011.

34 Dr. Patrick Sookhdeo, "Ideas Matter," in *Towards A Grand Strategy Against Terrorism*, eds. Christopher C. Harmon, A. N. Pratt, and Sebastian Gorka (New York: McGraw-Hill, 2010), 228–251.

35  For example, an August 2011 conversation with a senior manager at the Department of Homeland Security confirmed my sense that the analytical workforce is young or new to the field and rarely offers mastery of older terrorist groups. Yet in many cases those "old" cases introduced the very patterns that new analysts seek to understand in terrorism today.

36  A counterpart to terrorism studies is the field of counterintelligence. In 2009, John Lenczowski of IWP relayed to blogger Jeff Stein views on how counterintelligence work demands high levels of graduate school education. His informal thoughts, here paraphrased, include a broad knowledge of intelligence history and foreign cultures; the history of counterintelligence, not only in the U.S. but also in other countries; all the dimensions of counterintelligence, to include strategic deception; perceptions management, propaganda, and disinformation; covert (and even overt) political influence operations; strategic psychological operations; acts of political warfare; epistemological issues surrounding intelligence, including sensitivity to our own intellectual and cultural biases; the perceptions management efforts of foreign powers; the political and strategic cultures of foreign powers; the languages of those foreign powers; the categories and methods of counterintelligence analysis. April 7, 2009 "Spy Talk": http://blogs.cqrollcalll.com/spytalk/2009/04/wanted-dod-counterintelligence.html.

37  Habash lived on into "grand old man" status as PFLP's open political face. His second, Haddad, died earlier after many terrorist roles, included running the agent "Carlos."

38  Ernesto "Che" Guevara was a medical student in Argentina when he became radicalized and joined the revolution against the Batista regime in Cuba. After 1959 he continued his work for international communist revolution. He wrote a book on *Guerrilla Warfare* and diaries on his fights in the Congo (1965) and Bolivia (1966–1967). On June 14, 2011, the *Washington Times* reported that Cuba's Che Guevara Studies Center and an Australian publisher were releasing *Diary of a Combatant*, covering Che's arrival in Cuba in 1956 and subsequent action there.

39  The latter include anti-abortionists, who doubtless believe themselves idealists. Unrepresentative individuals out of this movement have shot doctors or clinic workers in several U.S. and Canadian cities.

40  Bell, *Cold Terror*, 43. See also Sean D. Hill and Richard H. Ward, eds., *Extremist Groups: An International Compilation* (Huntsville, TX: Sam Houston State University, 2002), 747–750.

41  On occasion, Al Qaeda leaders have offered diplomatic gambits (e.g., they told named European countries to withdraw troops from Muslim states if they would like peace—for the named government). Such offers are easy efforts at splitting the global alliance fighting Al Qaeda.

42  The United States Institute of Peace (USIP) has a new building near the State Department in Washington, D.C. At its conference on "Engaging Extremists," June 16, 2011, copies of its "Peacemaker's Toolkits" were distributed. The booklet on "Talking to Groups That Use Terror" (2011) is authored by Nigel Quinney and A. Heather Coyne; contributing scholars include Daniel Byman of Georgetown University and Guy Olivier Faure of the Sorbonne.

43 Jim Phillips, the Middle East expert at The Heritage Foundation in Washington, notes that European allies who formerly resisted sanctioning Iran have since 2009 been much more favorable to meeting this need; our e-mail exchange was in September 2011.

44 Bureau of Political-Military Affairs, Department of State, "MANPADS: Combating the Threat to Global Aviation from Man-Portable Air Defense Systems," July 27, 2011.

45 United Nations Security Council Resolution 1617 of 2005 mentions the problem, and three years before, UNSCR Resolution 1450 had noted the Arkia Israeli Airlines flight, narrowly missed by Al Qaeda missiles on November 28, 2002.

46 The literature on interrogation and torture now includes innumerable books and articles; one of the better columns of recent date is by Samuel G. Freedman, "'Zero Dark Thirty,' Through a Theological Lens," *New York Times*, February 23, 2013.

47 The classic history is Alistair Horne, *A Savage War of Peace, 1954–1962* (New York: Viking, 1977), which reappeared in paperback due to interest generated by the war starting in Iraq in 2003. The most instructive of the newer accounts, and one that attempts to justify torture, is by a French participant, then Major Paul Aussaresses, *The Battle of the Casbah: Terrorism and Counterterrorism in Algeria, 1955–1957*, trans. Robert L. Miller (New York: Enigma Books, 2002).

# 7

# WHAT CITIZENS CAN DO

Public approval of a powerful sort has enveloped the actions of passengers on the United Airlines flight above Pennsylvania on 9/11. At the cost of their lives, they took on Al Qaeda "musclemen," whose aim was crashing the flying bomb into the Capitol building in Washington, D.C. In a moment of crisis, these Americans—who had never met before—deliberated briefly, banded together, and charged down the aisle. These citizens thrust aside every natural and normal fear—and decades of past counsel by security personnel and airlines to comply quietly with hijackers' demands. They saved lives in Washington and also preserved an iconic and monumental building in the Capitol. On 9/11 these few became the newest "Minute Men"—worthy descendants of men with muskets at Concord and Lexington. In his book on sabotage and terrorism, David Tucker notes that two further Al Qaeda terrorists came to the same fate—being shoved to the floor by other passengers—in acts that later ended suicide air bombing dreams of Richard Reid and Umar Farouk Abdulmutallab.[1]

Sometimes less dramatically, yet more often, have been efforts by many other citizens in recent years to combat air piracy and other terrorism. For a time after the 1985 hijacking of Trans World Airlines (TWA) flight 847, Americans were deeply taken with the courage of purser Uli Derickson. This courageous young woman in flight uniform kept a calm manner and a firm backbone as she dealt with a fierce male team who repeatedly threatened her, beat passengers, and murdered a navy man. Her ability to speak German with several hijackers was a salve to tension at certain moments; she even acceded to their demands to sing German-language ballads. But she also (successfully) refused to do certain things as ordered, and she intervened against the beatings when she could. Later decorated for valor, Derickson showed how quiet resistance may lend nobility to a desperate scene, and how one person's courage can inspire everyone trapped in a crisis. There might have been a general massacre aboard TWA 847; that it never came was due, in part, to the coolness of professionals such as Uli Derickson. She and the equally impressive pilot, John Testrake,[2] have since died of natural causes. They deserve to be remembered.

At other times, U.S. citizens who were *not* trapped in a crisis have invited trouble by taking self-conscious and courageous acts. Suspecting terrorism, they have turned to modest instruments, such as a telephone or an anonymous letter, to work via appropriate authorities such as the police. Even that has risks: police files may "leak," and eager media may publish too much or neighbors may talk—making even such quiet acts risk exposure and retaliation. Yet such acts are building blocks of the civil society. Without citizen participation, counterterrorism will never be very effective.

The Yemeni American community living in Lackawanna, New York, is an example of a semi-exclusive demographic group. Such subsocieties are common throughout the U.S. and may be distinguished by religion, race, or other factors. When a few radicals penetrated this otherwise peaceable community a decade ago, bold young men began making the wrong-headed decision to join a purported "jihad." A half-dozen of these Americans of Yemeni descent flew to Southwest Asia for Al Qaeda training, and most of them did undergo that discipline in Afghanistan in 2001. A few months later, the right thing happened: a citizen of the Yemeni community in Lackawanna who knew this would only lead to bloodshed and oppressive inquiries in his or her community ventured to inform U.S. authorities anonymously.

The private citizen's letter began: "Two terrorists came to Lackawanna ... for recruiting the Yemenite youth." The letter gave names of recruits and details. "I cannot give you my name because I fear for my life," ended the two pages, unsigned. But it reached the authorities, who placed the names on an FBI watch list. That, in turn, allowed law enforcement to know when they would return from the training camps. Airport interrogations and surveillance that followed undergirded a successful legal prosecution. None of that might have happened without one careful citizen's letter. The alternative was terrorist mayhem. "Whoever sent it to us is a hero," said an FBI case officer later.[3]

A professor of English at Florida's Broward College is another such risk-taker and good citizen. He remains unnamed publicly—doubtless a sensible precaution—but when the time came he did the right thing, pre-empting a horrible attack. Hearing of an investigation into an Al Qaeda man named Adnan Shukrijumah, the professor recalled having him in a class. All students had been assigned presentations which were filmed for instructional purposes. The teacher accessed his tape and gave it to the FBI. With the pictures and audiotape the subject was identified as a "controller" for Najibullah Zazi and Zarein Ahmedzay, two more in a long line of plotters against the transit system under New York City. The professor's film greatly advanced the case against the plotters of a double-suicide bomb attack. Its many victims were to be typical Americans on the subway. One may gauge the sort of horrors such terrorists dream of by remembering the pictures of the successful underground attack in London in 2005.[4] The professor's film helped in a second way: it identified a man who had not been captured but was rising in Al Qaeda ranks; the FBI believes he is an operational planner. Now, at least, intelligence knows who to watch for.

For every time an average citizen takes a noble action and aids law enforcement, there are a dozen more instances in which the guardian of order is a public security officer, trained and paid to be discerning and decisive. When one of these quiet people with years of public service is killed by a criminal, droves of officials and civil servants leave city hall to join in the solemn motorcade and funeral. That is as it should be. Yet we would do well to think of these men and women while they are still alive and serving.

It was an obscure state trooper in Oklahoma to whom we owe the arrest of the Alfred P. Murrah Federal Building truck bomber, barely one hour after his attack. When Timothy McVeigh was caught on April 19, 1995, he had cleanly escaped the scene of his crime and would soon make it across the Kansas State line, perhaps never to be found. But on duty that day on the roads of Noble County, Oklahoma, was Charles J. Hanger, who stopped a moving Mercury Monarch without license plates. Under questioning at the roadside, the terrorist—a U.S. Army vet with no warrants outstanding or prior arrests—was remarkably calm, relaxed, and cooperative, as trial transcripts would show.

But then came a second clue, more important than the lack of tags. As McVeigh reached for his wallet to produce his driver's license, a slight bulge appeared underneath his windbreaker jacket—the bulge of a holster and pistol. The experienced officer guessed what it was.

Immediately, the two men began discussing that gun—for which there was no permit. "My weapon is loaded," said Timothy McVeigh. "So is mine," replied the officer. The terrorist was soon on his way to jail. But there was still no legal connection to the bomb that killed 168 Americans. That came later, in part because of Trooper Hanger's careful search through his car after unloading McVeigh—a routine the policeman kept so that nothing could ever be dropped by one suspect and later used as a weapon by another rider. Crumpled up under the seat where the right-wing extremist had been seated was the business card of Paulsen's Military Supply company, and on it were words including these: "TNT @ $5 a stick. Need more."[5] Charles Hanger's care with every part of his craft, especially his coolness while arresting a gunman, placed a mass murderer in the dock—and later in the electric chair.

A modest customs inspector named Diana Dean was inspecting cars on the passenger ferry crossing over from Canada into U.S. territory at Port Angeles, Washington, in late 1999. She had no reason to know that Ahmed Ressam, in the last car to leave the ferry, had "lit up" Canadian officials' computers on the other side of the water. Unfortunately, Canadian border authorities had earlier let Ressam *into* Canada and now also let him *out* ... so he arrived in the U.S. to meet Diana Dean. She had no way of knowing that Ressam was in a terrorist cell and was intent on driving south to Los Angeles to attack the international airport on behalf of the Algerian members of Al Qaeda. Her training, however, did allow her to notice this driver's nervousness, and she began questioning. When Ressam bolted from the car, the game was up. Inspectors found bomb components hidden in the wheel well—ingredients including the volatile chemical nitroglycerine.[6]

New Jersey trooper Robert Cieplensky found his intuitions aroused by the behavior of a Japanese tourist on April 12, 1988. When Yu Kikumura pulled into a turnpike rest stop, the trooper peered carefully into the car and did not like what he saw. Closer investigation revealed aluminum powder, ammonium nitrate, mercury, lead shot, and canisters to be fitted as bombs. The "tourist" had been jailed in

Europe for terrorism and had taken training in a Middle East camp. He was driving to a navy recruiting office in New York and had no plans to enlist. Instead, his bombs were to salute the second anniversary of the U.S. air raid on Libya on April 14, 1986. "Anniversary" attacks on that day in 1988 did hit Americans living in Italy, Spain, Costa Rica, Peru, and Colombia.[7] But nothing happened in New Jersey or New York because a smart public servant on highway patrol did his job well. Even in the national security studies field it seems few remember Robert Cieplensky. We should. A security expert who knows this story, Louis R. Mizell, Jr., observes that such routine traffic stops by police officers are "one of our most valuable counterterrorist weapons," catching 88 domestic or international terrorists during the years 1977 through 1997.[8]

The earnest citizen and the established authorities come together in new anti-terrorism education programs that encourage individual citizen reporting. These may go under the name "If You See Something, Say Something" injunction of the New York Metropolitan Transit Authority since 2002. Today the Department of Homeland Security is attempting to spread such programs to other localities, recognizing as they do that prestige cities are not alone as targets of Al Qaeda and other terrorists. Despite a mid-2010 flurry of activity by the Department of Homeland Security, the campaign has not reached many American citizens. AMTRAK, the national train system that is private yet dependent upon public funds, has also begun getting involved in the program. In some areas, auto drivers might see an electronic bulletin board with a 1–800 number for anti-terrorist calls, an excellent approach that should be expanded. The Pentagon's internal hallways sport posters—although that readership ranks last among those needing information, as most of those in uniform are already prepared to make the right call when occasion requires.

A second but tolerable problem with the "If You See Something, Say Something" program is that the public criticism of it tends to leave more impression than the initial request for information. Jokers or cynics discuss "turning in" every foreign tourist with a camera, and civil libertarians get indignant about each of us reporting on our neighbors as if we are all junior *Stasi* agents. Public figures have missed many opportunities to tender good advice in these policy and civics discussions, although George W. Bush did well, on the occasion of a speech, listing a half dozen or more "pre-emptions" of terrorist acts. A listener to that speech could tell how information from the public alerts the right authorities. Yet such exhortations to public involvement are rare from senior American politicians.

Judgment will always play a role in whether a citizen makes that phone call. And the quickness of a citizen's report of suspicious behavior is often *not* a priority—despite the excess enthusiasm on some roadside signs. Some thoughtful assessment of just what is in view or suspected makes sense—to make the report more valuable to authorities. Written details may prove invaluable. Just because a man-portable air defense weapon in terrorist hands is one of today's most pressing dangers, one ought not to call the Federal Aviation Authority about "a missile tube" in an airport taxi if, viewed from 70 or 80 yards away, it is more likely a set of golf clubs. Arab Americans and visiting relatives from abroad have every right to take a video of the elevators at the Washington Monument or the piers at Baltimore Harbor. It may be quite another thing if a local concessionaire sees the same party of young men the next day reshooting the scene, acting nervous or secretive, or handing the videotape or camera device over to a third party who is breaking away from the group.[9]

There is another rubric of citizen—in a distinctive and popular profession—who could play a vital role in discrediting terrorism but may be missing opportunities to help secure our nation: our media. Terrorism is about political influence and power; terrorists, even more than political scientists, fully understand the value of media coverage. When Americans were held hostage in the lengthy TWA 847 crisis of 1985, the Hezbollah and Amal gunmen staged press conferences and exhibited the strongest interest in how they were being portrayed.[10] The former German neo-Nazi Ingo Hasselbach tells of accepting big fees from TV and print reporters, German and foreign. At times, their deals explicitly included "acting" roles by the neo-Nazis. His published memoir explains how significant it was to have mainstream media lend "dignity" to his extremist movement.[11] Such attitudes and actions are well known to scholars of terrorism, who have expressed concerns similar to Margaret Thatcher's about the "oxygen" that media supplies to terrorism.[12] Since all of our citizens should be opposed to terrorism, this applies to reporters, media officials, and news executives. Their work sometimes seems to favor release of a hot story at the expense of the public good. Some stories clearly glamorize terrorism. Is there a "right" way to cover terror incidents? Can our media report responsibly on terrorism without amplifying the gunman's message? The answer is "Yes."

Responsible TV stations and the better newspapers recognized the problem a generation ago. Bales of press stories and some careful books documented the relationship between news coverage and terrorist aspirations to influence large audiences. Some media organizations established professional codes for proper coverage of terrorist incidents. The *New York Times* is an example of a newspaper that has several times leaked important intelligence about terrorism and counterterrorism, but also allows open debate about such reporting in its letters columns or in postings by its ombudsman. The media's self-written codes for appropriate reporting may or may not be followed; they are sometimes ignored when an editor obtains an irresistible "exclusive." But the idea of the codes make sense, and they could help everyone in media work to remember their responsibilities. In my view, correspondents must be citizens first and reporters second.

The media's professional codes should implant these principles, among others. First, never make payment for access to extremists. Second, balance terrorists' "air time" with rebuttals, critique, and the same sharp questioning reporters pride themselves on when speaking with their own politicians. Third, show as much interest in terrorism's victims as in the gunmen who hurt them. While obsessive coverage of a family's agony during a hostage case may be tasteless and "raise the price of the hostage," coverage of the victims *after* the crisis may be helpful and certainly it may be just. Yet, often this goes missing. Fourth, report not just on the words and acts of terrorist leaders but also on their flaws—for example, criminal backgrounds, character defects, shoddy political motives, messianic fanaticisms, the financial interest many have in the terrorist criminal "lifestyle," etc. The media sometimes glamorizes terrorists, but it has a moral duty to do the opposite. Fifth, reporters, editors, and producers are and must be citizens. Instead of a credo that emphasizes "news" of any kind, peer competition, and the absence of "value judgments," media personnel should weight their choices toward sane politics, emotional balance, the value of life, and the contrast between these qualities with the moral ugliness of terrorism—which is deliberate harm of the innocent for political shock.

Terrorism, by definition, concerns public affairs. What is needed is that all of us, as citizens, be alert to how we might better serve the public interest.

## Notes

1 David Tucker, *Illuminating the Dark Arts of War: Terrorism, Sabotage, and Subversion in Homeland Security and the New Conflict* (New York: Continuum International Publishing Group, 2012), 247–248.

2 Captain John Testrake wrote a memoir, *Triumph Over Terror on Flight 847* (Old Tappan, NJ: Fleming H. Revell Co, 1987). It says little of Uli Derickson, but her courageous actions were reported at the time.

3 Quoted in Temple-Raston, *The Jihad Next Door*, 124.

4 CNN, August 6, 2010, in a story highlighting the work of the FBI's Brian LeBlanc.

5 McVeigh carried a .45 pistol loaded with "Black Talon" ammunition that would mushroom when striking a body—a devastating combination of size and shape. Details of the arrest are available at "Timothy McVeigh Trial: Documents Relating to McVeigh's Arrest and the Search of His Vehicle," at http://law2unke.edu/faculty/projects/fttrials/mcveigh/mcveigharrest.html.

6 Apart from published accounts, this section relies upon my discussion with former U.S. Attorney John McKay of Washington State, who handled some of the appeals matters in the Ressam case.

7 Department of State, *Patterns of Global Terrorism: 1988* (Washington, D.C.: GPO, 1989), 45–46.

8 Louis R. Mizelle, Jr., *Target U.S.A.: The Inside Story of the New Terrorist War* (New York: John Wiley & Sons, 1998), 145. It is unfortunate that Mizelle's excellent book is unknown to many today.

9 Illustrating the challenges of judgment, the Marine Corps' Carl Shelton had this mystery in northwest Washington, D.C., in April 2002. He and an associate had their suspicions aroused in the tense months just after 9/11. Colonel Shelton was visiting a friend in D.C. who mentioned his irritation over trash management by a group of eight Middle Eastern males, non-Americans, renting a neighboring apartment. The eight kept to themselves rigorously, with blinds closed. Yet their wariness was odd; they also received many late-night visitors. One such was a man with Canadian license plates who first told Shelton's friend he was "lost" but then stayed overnight with the group. The suspicious resident discussed the facts with the Muslim landlady in a conversation occasioned by the group's habit of putting their trash in other residents' receptacles. Shelton, a force protection officer for a distant military base, recommended quietly monitoring this—as a possible security issue. This proved important: often, on the mornings just before trash pickup, the group of eight distributed their own material in the disposal cans of other residents on that street. Both the irritated resident and his friend Shelton next made telephone

calls, one to the Washington Metropolitan Police and the other to the FBI. Two months later, the resident noted late-night pickups of certain bagged trash along the street by an unusual van with government plates. In August 2002, the apartment was vacated. The landlady confirmed that authorities had come to question the eight residents at length. Shelton and his D.C. ally judge these events to show the value of the counsel: "If You See Something, Say Something." Here were two sensible citizens—not petty meddlers—dealing well with an awkward neighborhood problem that may have disguised a larger matter of mutual security. They neither over-reacted nor failed to act. They warned authorities, but only after sensibly observing behavior for long enough to form a judgment.

10  John Testrake's book (see note 2) has details. More generally, terrorists' obsession with their own press is a familiar pattern; Ulrike Meinhof and many others were relentless keepers of clipping files.

11  Ingo Hasselbach with Tom Reiss, *Fuhrer-Ex: Memoirs of a Former Neo-Nazi* (New York: Random House, 1996).

12  During the late 1970s and early 1980s there were books and monographs about media and terrorism. A newer and thoughtful handling of the relationship, which also includes references to work by Walter Laqueur and Paul Wilkinson, is a book chapter, "The Media and the Terrorist" by Reuters editor Mark Trevelyan in *Toward A Grand Strategy Against Terrorism*, op. cit.

# 8

# HOW OTHER TERRORIST GROUPS HAVE BEEN DEFEATED

A terrorist group has no natural lifespan. Some researchers have tried to calculate the average life years for terror groups, but the figures yielded serve neither the citizen nor police science. The willpower of the terrorist leader, chance, and the role of government intervention may throw out any mathematical prospects for how long a terrorist group will thrive. Thus, in social science it is misleading, if not a blunder, to write that terrorist groups have an average lifespan—although several scholars have. We should understand the lessons of terrorism's history unprejudiced, not seeking either optimism or pessimism in statistics. These brutish organizations are human, and dynamic, and they may perish from at least a half-dozen very different causes, or a combination of them. As victims, enemies, and eventually victors, we American citizens must understand the contest, fight, and direct our energies well, with a strategy.

Several of the Marxist-Leninist models offer perspective on this question of longevity and how terror groups end. Malaysian "Communist Terrorists," as they were called by the British, are usually said to have been beaten in 12 years, between 1948 and 1960. And in most respects they were, although the insurgents' leader, a serious Maoist, refused to acknowledge was defeat and clung to tenets of protracted warfare, hanging on along the Thai–Malay border until the end of the 1980s. By contrast, the Symbionese Liberation Army of California was born, lived, and defeated, all within four years. They had different strategies, and very different longevity, but similar fates: defeat.

The right end of the ideological spectrum offers equal ranges. In 1980, three bombings in Europe convinced hasty analysts that a neo-fascist wave of terror had arrived. One of these, a bomb at Munich's Oktoberfest, was laid by the "Hoffman Military Sports Group," which enjoyed access to Middle East training camps. But that group vanished in three years. By contrast, the hard white racists of America's Ku Klux Klan first formed in the immediate post-Civil War period, carried on generation after generation, and even under fierce federal pressures survive today and drive on toward their 150th anniversary, a benchmark coming in 2015.

Terror groups—and insurgencies systematically using terror—are neither doomed to a short life nor assured of a long one merely because they have strategies of "attrition" or "protracted war." So, what determines their longevity? Duration over many years is often the result of these factors: *strong leadership, deep pockets, or outside support.* Terrorism is and has always been a test of wills, and a willful leader, even one so politically unpalatable as Abu Nidal, the Palestinian nationalist leader of "Black June," may survive as a terrorist leader for decades—and he did. Money can allay many of the leadership's concerns about the future,[1] encourage recruiting, and guarantee a flow of weapons and available places of refuge. When groups such as FARC in Colombia and the Taliban in Afghanistan make hundreds of millions of dollars per year in cocaine and opium, any assessment of their longevity must be generous; they may need little popular support and no foreign state support. Or, perhaps outside support is essential, in which case its withdrawal will be fatal. Insurgencies with safe-havens across a border have a far greater chance of survival. A terrorist group such as the Palestine Islamic Jihad might be teetering on the edge of collapse, were it not for the absolutely reliable patronage of the state of Iran, year after year after year.

There are at least five categories for understanding the demise of terrorist groups.[2]

Force is one way in which terrorists come to their end. "The Order," a neo-Nazi group led by Robert Matthews, moved for months like a criminal pinball up and down roadways of the Pacific Northwest, netting hundreds of thousands of dollars in robberies of banks and armored cars. They were aiming to create a "whites only" zone within American borders. But many errors in planning and execution translated into many arrests. As police closed in on Matthews, the charismatic leader opted for an exchange of gunfire. He died in a burning house on Whidbey Island in Washington State, the unexpected funeral pyre observed by scores of heavily armed law enforcement personnel from local to national levels. Similar uses of force by scores of SWAT team experts and other police account for the demise of other groups, such as the Symbionese Liberation Army that captured newspaper heiress Patty Hearst.

After many arrests, government commandos took just moments in 1997 to destroy what remained of MRTA, or "Tupac Amaru," Peruvian militants whose members included New Yorker Lori Berenson— who has been excused from jail for a visit to the U.S. but who remains on parole in Peru.

Beyond such discrete uses of force there are larger military campaigns, such as the one Sri Lankan armed forces concluded in May 2009, crushing the popular, fanatical, foreign-trained guerrillas of the LTTE Tamil Tigers. In that unfortunate case, force was required to finally conclude a fight that had for decades resisted solution by patience, negotiation, and formal cease-fires. Latin America offers older cases, and so does Turkey, in which military coups permitted suppression of terrorism before returning authority to civil authorities. Canada, proudly liberal, judged it could only deal with the Quebecois leftist terror campaign peaking in the late 1960s by proclaiming martial law. When that earth-shaking decision was made in 1970, the violence was quickly quelled.

A second and smaller category of terrorist defeats is decapitation. That option fascinates several senior U.S. officials now that bin Laden and some other Al Qaeda leaders are jailed or dead. Over time and history, "decapitation" has usually been a mere dream for frustrated state forces. And, yet, decapitation of revolutionary organizations *has* occurred in a few cases. One example, a century ago, is the clever capture of Emilio Aguinaldo, the Filipino nationalist leader; when he was seized via U.S. trickery in 1901, his insurrection collapsed. An excellent and recent example is the capture of Sendero Luminoso creator Abimael Guzman, since 1992 jailed in Peru. A few hundreds remain of "Shining Path," but they are ineffectual and no serious threat to the democratic order.

In a more qualified way one may learn from the Kurdistan Workers' Party (PKK). This separatist movement, which once boasted as many as 40,000 cadre, was stunned into immobility by the capture of its monomaniacal head, Abdullah Ocalan. The PKK was almost impotent from 1999 through 2003, changing its name and losing its way. That half-decade bought breathing space for our NATO ally, the Republic of Turkey. It is also notable that the first cause of defeat discussed above—force—helped to set up this second, the 1999 decapitation. After years of Turkish complaints through proper channels to Damascus, it was Turkish troop movements threatening Syria that caused the latter to expel Ocalan from his long-term safe-haven behind the Syrian borders. That compelled the PKK leader to flee to Africa, but his flight unwittingly set up his later rendition back to Turkey, where he remains in jail, busying himself during 2013 with "peace negotiations" with the regime in Ankara.

Third, history suggests that some insurgencies using terror, and some smaller terrorist groups not able to qualify as real insurgencies, lose to a state's good grand strategy. The state prevails over the terrorists through an intelligent design that includes willpower, patience, and cooperative effort between military, law enforcement, and intelligence personnel. The Red Army Faction (RAF) is certainly famous—and the recent German film about them called *The Baader Meinhof Complex* is instructive. The organization has not much affected German life since 1977. In our day, the RAF remains fascinating; but the only news is of releases coming after long jail terms. Birgit Hogefeld—one of the many females in the group—has been released from jail; she had killed Americans and Germans a generation ago. Verena Becker has been on trial for killing a prosecutor 35 years ago. Historians pore through what remains of the feared *Stasi* files, which document the RAF's freedoms of action in Communist East Germany; other state supporters are long gone. But it is not too late to laude the West German republic for its patience, its willpower, its science, and its careful application of law. At a few points, force was applied—including one strike by the special border police of GSG-9. All of these were parts of a winning design for defeating the RAF in a long campaign.

"A pacific way," or entry into peaceful politics, is a fourth route available to militants. The pathways out of terrorism have been studied by scholars such as Paul Wilkinson and Stanford's Martha Crenshaw, a specialist in group decision-making. Ascent out of violence may be very individual and personal; cases have been examined by psychologist John Horgan. It is notable that many a choice to quit is made in the face of protracted state pressure over numerous years and the natural fatigue inherent in the underground life. That judgment should not be thought merely a personal change of mind; pursuit by authorities may well shape the terrorist's mind.

El Salvador's guerrilla front FMLN was no coalition of enthused land reformers; it was a martial alliance of ideologues and extremists that Fidel Castro and others cobbled together following the successful precedent in Sandinista Nicaragua. The Salvadoran insurgents aimed to conquer as Daniel Ortega's organization had done next door. The Farabundo Marti National Liberation Front waged war with some successes for years before declaring a "final offensive" against San Salvador in 1989. But their offensive failed—as guerrilla assaults on cities often have. Soviet bloc backers were disappearing. The troubled state of El Salvador survived, despite years of dreadful economic and human damage, due to the resilience of the Salvadoran people, the courage of their democratic politicians, the stamina of sectors as different as the army and the newspapers, and billions of dollars in U.S. economic, military, and other aid. The war was brought to a formal close in January 1992 under United Nations supervision.[3] This good conclusion had also been prepared by elaborate diplomacy, including the mediation of friendly countries: the Contadora Group led by Mexico and then the Esquipulas Peace Agreement championed by Costa Rica. Today the FMLN is a highly successful mainstream left-wing political party and controls the executive branch. Latin American variants on such a turn toward democratic ways may be studied in the older cases of M-19 in Colombia, and the Tupamaros of Uruguay, two terrorist groups that met defeat at state hands yet carried on through the initiative of many members, individuals who have since enjoyed successful political careers in the open democratic process.

A fifth way in which terrorist campaigns conclude is far less pleasant to contemplate: the terrorist group wins. Communist organizations have done so by combining terrorism with other overt and covert political tools. Their successes begin with Bolshevism in Russia in 1917 and continue up through the Khmer Rouge triumph of 1975 in Cambodia, and Vietnamese success the same year next door. Algerian FLN (National Liberation Front) nationalists routinely used terror, as well as other tools and methods, and thus compelled France to leave their lands in 1962. Enamored with the Algerian FLN model, and its combinations of terrorism and other means, Yasser Arafat ran his Palestine Liberation Organization (PLO) with a finesse many did not fully appreciate. He trained and deployed guerrillas and terrorists, controlled the massive outside donations to his movement, emerged in honor as a speaker at the UN General Assembly in 1974, and went on to establish a Palestine Authority (PA) "statelet" in the West Bank. It may be small, weak, and troubled, but the PA has international and American support and is likely to prevail in some form. The fall of 2011 found the nationalists driving for UN formal recognition, which won approval by the UN General Assembly during the next year. To take another recent example: from 1997 to 1999, Kosovar insurgents and terrorists initiated violence that led to the creation of a nascent state Kosovo Liberation Army (KLA). The North Atlantic Treaty Organization helped to promote these efforts and now Kosovo is another independent state born from the wreckage of the mid 20th-century state of Yugoslavia.[4]

Closer scholarly research must one day illuminate the phenomenon of "partial success" by terrorists. Many insurgencies, despite bloody hands, have used well-calculated combinations of methods to rise to positions of real consequence—if also short of full strategic success. Nepal's Maoist insurgents, under a gifted duo of leaders, opened war in 1996. Fighting raged for the next decade, but so did their careful war of underground politics and their overt contest of diplomacy and politicking. Their success may not be complete. But their Communist party emerged as the dominant one inside the whole of the Nepalese parliament, and in recent years, each of the two top Maoist leaders has served in the country's post of prime minister. One of them made a state visit to New York City. The model is also in use half a world away, in the Middle East, by Hamas and Hezbollah, Islamist fundamentalist sects turned mainstream political actors. Both have strong electoral powers yet rightly remain on the U.S. terrorism lists.

The natural interest in lessons to be learned from such case studies must compete with the knowledge that each country, and each war, is unique in some respects. What we most wish to know is: what will be the fate of Al Qaeda? This author has long argued that the world community *would* prevail over Al Qaeda but that it would demand new and sustained efforts.[5] Perhaps now it would be useful to examine the prospects for Al Qaeda according to each of the five alternatives discussed above.

Force was mentioned first and is very often a factor, given that terrorism is about power and politics. Al Qaeda may be doomed, but it is a fierce worldwide organization, and in 2001 it was probably history's most powerful terrorist group ever. It had then and has now two distinguishable centers of gravity from which power and movement flow:[6] *strong leadership* and *strong doctrine*. The importance of ideas to Al Qaeda principals and followers means that force alone by a U.S.-led coalition is not a likely victor. Now the U.S. and its allies have killed or captured many leaders and second-tier leaders—half of them, according to President Obama, speaking on June 22, 2011. This attrition has meant strong progress against the first center of power. The movement's second engine, ideological strength, has not been broken, and efforts to wear it down are going badly, as indicated in the pages above. That is our assessment of the fight with Al Qaeda and the broader Islamist terror movement in regard to the use of force.

The second way that terrorist groups end—decapitation—deserves some consideration, especially with bin Laden gone. Defense Secretary Leon Panetta seemed enamored with this manner of defeating Al Qaeda.[7] The president and some other officials and analysts sometimes seemed to share his hope. But Mr. Panetta left the Pentagon probably without ever seeing as much as a new unstaged photo of the reclusive Al Qaeda leader Ayman al Zawahiri. The larger problem is that *no individual is quite as significant as the ideology,* which can continue recruiting and motivating. Dr. Al Zawahiri could perish or be captured and it could be that another commander and veteran would take the overall lead. After all, the Al Qaeda camps in Afghanistan trained thousands, year after year, and hundreds remain at large.

If we jump ahead to the fourth option, is there any prospect of Al Qaeda folding into pacific political life? Very little. Terrorists may consider this option when they are near to defeat—but Al Qaeda is not defeated. The next difficulty is that "going democratic" means "surrender" for most Al Qaeda fanatics; they would refuse, and many would prefer to die fighting. It is thus empty to hope for a "mellowing" of Al Qaeda; their cadre must be captured or wounded in battle or killed. Only certain individuals will be amenable to de-radicalization, and far fewer of those will meld into pacific politics. For Al Qaeda, even imprisonment may not be a solution. Yemen and Afghanistan have been the scenes of large-scale prison breaks. Washington, for its part, has many recent examples of sheer folly to study, as some of the Al Qaeda and Taliban men released from Guantanamo Bay have returned to active terrorism.

One can say with conviction that the fifth option, terrorist victory, is not possible in Al Qaeda's case—except in narrow places under perhaps different names. We might, for example, see a province of Yemen or a township in Pakistan under the *sharia*, administered by personnel of Al Qaeda. But too many anti-Al Qaeda governments are on notice, and Al Qaeda today lacks the strength to take over, manage, and govern any country. Nor would neighboring states allow such a new state. So whether we consider the most likely prospects, or merely eliminate the impossible, Al Qaeda will not win. It will lose to our rather ungainly grand strategy, with its mix of many efforts at home and its expansive foreign work with so many international partners and combatant countries. Winston Churchill quipped that "There is only one thing worse than fighting with allies, and that is fighting without them." We have many allies, and some may be tougher than we are. What we'll most need from our partners in the next years is not more troops in Iraq or Afghanistan, but more arrests, convictions, intelligence sharing, and good ideas for discrediting Al Qaeda. We need good grand strategy—option three.

This war is a new one, and different, but not entirely so. Like all others it involves the use of power for national defense and other political purposes. And some very familiar concepts of strategy are guiding what the U.S. is now doing against Al Qaeda. "Containment," the famous post-1945 doctrine that evolved for preventing further Soviet progress westward, has checked the growth of Al Qaeda. We have built a worldwide alliance. Once, Al Qaeda had members in 60 countries and training camps in a handful. Today such numbers must be down by half or more. And our "containment" efforts have a working partner: "attrition."

Attrition is the opposite of "annihilation" and is a strategy recognized for wearing away the willpower of an opponent by diminishing his numbers of troops. Thousands of Taliban and Al Qaeda were killed, captured, or swept off battlefields in late 2001, and it is a rare event when they successfully challenge any major military installation—in

Southwest Asia or anywhere else. Two deadly suicide attacks on ships occurred, but the last of these came in 2004. Nuclear procurement efforts were soaking up Al Qaeda wealth in 2001; today there is probably no budget for such expensive bombs. Ten years ago, Al Qaeda had two famed and accomplished leaders; now one of these is dead. This is attrition—our coalition is winning by erosion, rather than annihilation. The U.S. and its allies can grind down Al Qaeda and its lethal partners. It is not the perfect strategy, and it continues to demand our patience, but it is working. We have performed rather well against Al Qaeda Central, even if not so well against the newer manifestations of Islamist extremism in Mali, Iraq, Yemen, and other zones.

Attrition strategies have enjoyed such different forms of victory as U.S. frontier forces defeating late 19th-century Indians, Filipino republicans defeating the Hukbalahap Communist insurgents in the early 1950s, and German security forces grinding down the Baader-Meinhofs of a generation ago. Today Spain has worn down the Basque ETA. It has for decades battered the Basque militants with every legal, political, intelligence, and police tool it has, to include political concessions and thousands of arrests, and ETA is a mere shadow of its former self. The attrition of decades has ground down not only ETA's leaders but also the second- and third-tier cadre, hundreds of whom are in jail. The long fight has also worn down political supporters. The ETA group survives but is sickly.[8]

A final question dogs the matter of Al Qaeda's fate. Is their ferocious religious doctrine so different as to, one, make historical lessons useless, or, two, doom our counterterrorism efforts? No. On both accounts, no.

Anarchism, also, was a fierce doctrine. Hundreds and hundreds of devotees to it, and victims of it, died between 1880 and 1920 in the world's northern hemisphere. The anarchists were ideological zealots with the kind of strength that made them tough debaters, patient jail birds, gunmen for hire at low wages or none, and persons inured to risk and hunger and life underground. They played pursuit games with some of the modern era's nastiest security forces, such as the Tsarist Okrana. They were not afraid to carry primitive dynamite bombs—even though some detonated prematurely. Some anarchists relished their public trials, made hot speeches, and went to the gallows proudly. Their numbers included idealistic grandmotherly figures, hard young men, well-known public intellectuals, and unprincipled criminals out of common jails.

It is instructive to recall how the anarchists lost. Over time, counterterrorist forces rallied against them. Governments learned to use the law to deny their visas or block their meetings. Detectives trailed the public speakers, wore them down, and built intelligence files for eventually deporting them. Countries assembled at international conferences to coordinate legal strategies and policing. The U.S. had no national database for anarchists and no national police force to arrest them; but it gained on the problem in creating today's Federal Bureau of Investigation. Russia, once roused, policed up all the anarchists it could find, first using Tsarist police and then, with more definitive results, the nascent Cheka (later called the KGB). The lessons of the global anti-anarchist campaign are important because they show that even a strange and empowering ideological doctrine *can* be defeated. Armed anarchists disappeared, and were almost unseen for decades, even if they are now re-growing in a few places.[9]

## Our Way Ahead

In the contest with Al Qaeda and its allies, the United States has come far and generally done well. Now the way ahead is along a bridge built with many interconnected cables. To defeat the widely ranging Islamist extremist movement, there must be multiple and strong strands, interwoven into grand strategy.

Public diplomacy is among the most important of these strands. Washington cannot linger about for another decade. We have hoped— as we should—that wise Muslim voices on the other side will do the most to quell the brutish appeal of Islamist terrorists. Established countries—such as NATO members and states forming the much larger Organization of the Islamic Conference—must help the world community to create and maintain political momentum against Al Qaeda, until it wins the ideological battle against the enemy doctrine. The enemy is a movement to be argued with (not only an organization) and thus far the United States has been too defensive-minded, and nearly devoid of new political arguments and ideas. Many other countries are also neglecting their duties to defend the innocent—terrorism's favorite targets. The world must not be as it was in 1890 or

1895 when countries gaped at anarchist terrorists with incomprehension and had little system for responding. We should be, we will be, like the world in 1910 or 1920—when states turned to trading intelligence out of mutual interest, policing up each other's violent émigrés, and taking the other common measures necessary across the affected countries. Thus resisted, anarchism lost its violent spirit.

Al Qaeda commenced in 1988, making this its third decade of international terrorism. Our decade will likely be Al Qaeda's last as a directed and mass-killing organization. Alternates, factions, and spin-offs will survive or develop, but Al Qaeda as a central core may soon be broken. This is a global campaign, and success will not depend directly upon more, or less, U.S. troops in Iraq or Afghanistan. Al Qaeda will be beaten by grand strategy. That must include effective public diplomacy to discredit Islamism and bolster democratic alternatives. Certainly the grand strategy has featured, and must continue to feature, international partnerships; the will of democratic governments and the diverse contributions of their peoples; the spreading overseas of laws against material support to terrorism and continued efforts to track terrorists' funds; countermeasures against terrorist hate speech; enhanced intelligence work; devoted policing that includes both new help from Interpol and member countries' established SWAT teams; and, of course, all manner of conventional and unconventional military forces.

The world community worked against and outlasted the anarchists and their semi-autonomous cells, charismatic leaders, and learned propagandists of a century ago. NATO countries beat down *all* the indigenous communist terrorist cells of the late 1960s and the 1970s, despite their proven fervor and generous outside donors and easy safe-havens. The United States defeated the right-wing threat inside this republic after that threat showed itself repeatedly in the 1980s and 1990s. Now comes Islamist fanaticism, an ugly mix of old and new, a threat doctrine expressed (like all terrorism) by the deliberate targeting of the innocent for shock and political impact. For living Americans, this is a third wave of terrorism. Like the past terrorist waves, this one will break against the rock of good and free government, supported by a sober and determined citizenry.

This is our history in the making, *our* making.

## Notes

1 The rather well-researched 2010 French mini-series on "Carlos" the Jackal (Venezuelan communist Ilich Ramirez Sanchez) lays dangerous emphasis on money as a motivator of his small group (which was a partner of the Popular Front for the Liberation of Palestine). Over and over again in this film, decision-making is influenced by who is paying and how much, for a given attack. By the time Carlos is seized in Khartoum and rendered off to a Paris jail, some of his older sponsors deride him as a mere mercenary.

2 My rubric here was the basis of public lectures in 2003 and more in 2004, including a published version at The Heritage Foundation on May 19. There followed presentations to Andrew Marshall's Office of Net Assessment in the Pentagon, universities, and our National Counterterrorism Center. An example of early 2006 work is still on the website of the Woodrow Wilson Center for Scholars, Washington, D.C.: "How Terrorist Groups End," webcast of March 20. 2006 (Spring) saw Cambridge University Press offer my relevant pages on "What History Suggests about Terrorism and its Future" in *The Past as Prelude*, edited by military historians Williamson Murray and Richard Sinnreich.

3 Telephone interviews of July 2011 with Kim Holmes and Ray Walser, former State Department officials who worked on these issues in government service.

4 The KLA example is suggested by Thomas R. Mockaitis, *Resolving Insurgencies* (Carlisle Barracks, PA: Strategic Studies Institute, June 2011), 22–24. Mockaitis's monograph creates categories different from mine; his four are: insurgent victories; government victories; degenerate insurgencies; state success through co-option.

5 "How Al Qaeda May End," Backgrounder, no. 1760 (Washington, D.C.: The Heritage Foundation, May 19, 2004).

6 Language here about centers of gravity comes from the Carl von Clausewitz treatise *On War*.

7 *Washington Post*, July 10, 2011.

8 Harmon, *Orbis*, note 11, Chapter 4.

9 In the Spain of the 1930s there were armed anarchists—to name an exception. In 2011, *Commentary* magazine had an article asking about "The Return of Anarchism," while *The Journal of Counterterrorism and Homeland Security International* had a feature on the internationalization of the new anarchist violence.

# AFTERWORD

This manuscript was completed before newspapers such as *The Guardian* and the *New York Times* began publishing revelations based upon tens of thousands of documents stolen from the U.S. National Security Agency by contractor Edward Snowden. Most Americans, including this author, have not been able to see the documents, so firm judgments cannot yet be made. It does appear, however, that there will be an impact upon themes set down in this book.

Most voters have largely accommodated a limited degree of governmental intrusiveness, especially after the USA PATRIOT Act swept through our Congress with forceful approval after 9/11, as one way to prevent terrorist murderers. Perhaps our older citizens know from experience that democracies take emergency measures under pressure of war. Young voters, for their part, may be accustomed already to the new-fashioned idea of our own "exposure" on-line and the liberties that takes with personal information. But Americans are now questioning these assumptions, given the apparent extent of the new electronic data-gathering. While not the same as surveillance, the newest practices come close, and records kept now might be used by government indefinitely into our future. Almost no American believes that making an overseas phone call should initiate a record in government files or that private emails should be archived or accessed by intelligence services without appropriate oversight.

Secondly, the Snowden disclosures are deeply offensive to allies, and the damage may be broad enough to deter certain levels of future cooperation. This book argues that foreign partners and allies are keys to our success against international terrorism; if that is true, our government risks much by jeopardizing the trust of such partners. The Snowden revelations have undermined relations even with intimates in NATO such as France and Germany. More such troubles may be announced in our newspapers at any time.

Is there reason to tolerate the deep levels of intrusiveness alleged to exist? There is probably only one reason: the existence of a state of war. As a people, via our representatives, we have declared ourselves to be at war with Al Qaeda and its affiliates and those responsible for 9/11. That harsh reality accounts for why we may hold foreign nationals in Guantanamo, why certain forms of hazard pay or combat pay are awarded to our soldiers, how we set national and Pentagon priorities, and a dozen other important things. The question of government intrusiveness is but one more way in which the core question arises: we are either at war, or we declare ourselves to be at peace and reliant upon law enforcement and other non-martial mechanisms.

In a speech May 23, 2013, President Obama asked whether the September 2001 authorization for the use of force should be maintained or revised. He hinted strongly that change may come, and yet he did not recommend any or choose a new policy. There are great legal, moral, physical, and political consequences to being at war today; there will be dramatic change if we should declare an end. That decision would please those weary of "the long war" as well as many others who are guided by the North Star of the 4th amendment on privacy. But the decision could strip us of many defenses. It would mean a new legal quandary about the leaders and followers in Al Qaeda. The decision will instantly produce justifiable pressures to release the enemies we detained under conditions of war. The decision would quietly alter our foreign relations and shift our focus away from hostile non-state actors and sub-state enemies. In my own view, with Al Qaeda and its alliance still operational, it is at best irrational to unilaterally close this campaign. Nor have we yet decided how to proceed against the fierce ideology that motivates terrorists in the Islamist international. It is too early ... even though we all wish to see the time come.

Quantico, Virginia
November 2013

# ADDITIONAL RESOURCES

*Department of Defense. Joint Publication 3-26, Counterterrorism.*
*Washington, D.C., November 2009: www.defense.gov.*
> In large part a product of George W. Bush administration officials, the report was signed during the Obama administration and is very useful for seeing the problem the way our Pentagon sees it.

*Department of State. Country Reports on Terrorism: 2012.*
*Washington, D.C., 2013: www.state.gov.*
> Despite the occasional carping from academics, this is our government's best openly published periodical on how the terrorism fight is going, with details on individuals, groups, trends, and how our foreign partners work with us (or do not!). See also Department of State's "Travel Advisories" on the website before going overseas.

*Europol/European Union. TE-SAT 2013 [Terrorism Situation and Trend Report],*
*Annual.*
*See: http://europa.eu.*
> While not as detailed as the Germans' annual from their Office for the Protection of the Federal Constitution, the report looks at most of Europe and terrorist patterns therein. It should be better known to Americans as a useful information source, especially given American interests in NATO.

*Christopher C. Harmon, Andrew N. Pratt, and Sebastian Gorka. Toward A Grand*
*Strategy against Terrorism.*
*New York: McGraw-Hill's Higher Education Division, 2010.*
> This textbook for upper-level education is not focused on the Al Qaeda campaign. It grew out of Colonel A. N. Pratt's unique Program on Terrorism and Security Studies of the George C. Marshall European Center for Security Studies, a long-running outreach partnership of the United States and Germany.

Rex A. Hudson. *Who Becomes a Terrorist and Why.*
*Guilford, CN: Lyons Press, 1999.*
> This undated, outstanding little paperback is the commercial print of a 1999 Library of Congress report. It deftly summarizes many schools of thought on the nature of terrorism, as well as profiling many older leaders and groups. It does not attempt to cover counterterrorism.

*Interpol [International Policing Agency].*
*See: www.Interpol.int.*
> The website is an invaluable resource for what others in the international intelligence and law-enforcement communities are watching and working on in terrorism. Dozens of other kinds of crime concern Interpol, which has come new to this contest with terrorists.

*Jane's Intelligence Review.*
> This monthly periodical is the single best open source for sophisticated analysis of evolving terrorist threats, with many in-depth articles on named groups or networks. For example, a special issue in the fall of 2010 detailed the affiliate organizations of Al Qaeda. But the journal is expensive; one should ask at a good library.

*Michael B. Kraft and Edward Marks. U.S. Government Counterterrorism: A Guide to Who Does What.*
*Boca Raton, FL: CRC Press, 2012.*
> Three hefty volumes offer extensive coverage of recent and current governmental issues and policy choices. Included are partial texts of many official speeches and papers. The set has been done with care and there is no wasted space.

*Walter Laqueur. The Age of Terrorism, 2nd edition.*
*Boston, MA: Little, Brown & Co., 1988.*
> Knowing many languages, and a learned student of innumerable terrorist groups, this scholar is as good as he is easy to read. Like Martha Crenshaw at Stanford or Paul Wilkinson, who recently died in Scotland, Laqueur is a master whose works over many years have educated most of the scholars now in this field.

*National Commission on Terrorist Attacks upon the United States. The 9/11 Commission Report. Washington, D.C.: Government Printing Office, July 2004.*
> This document has few peers as a study in counterterrorism and its failures. It has profoundly shaped our policy and strategy.

*James Phillips.*
> An expert on Afghanistan and the Middle East, this gentleman's short articles, longer "Backgrounders," and congressional testimony for The Heritage Foundation in Washington, D.C., have been thoughtful and reliable sources of fact and opinion for three decades.

*David Tucker. Illuminating the Dark Arts of War: Terrorism, Sabotage, and Subversion in Homeland Security and the New Conflict.*
New York: Continuum International Publishing Group, 2012.
Tucker's valuable books reflect many years in the Foreign Service and the Pentagon and they challenge conventional wisdom.

*United Nations.*
See: www. un.org/en.
The UN's websites on peace keeping operations and terrorism are useful. For example, the UN has a Counterterrorism Committee named for its resolution number 1627 that tracks violations of its convention on fighting the financing of terrorism.

*White House. National Security Strategy: May 2010.*
*White House. National Strategy for Counterterrorism: June 2011.*
The two Barack Obama White House releases are important to understanding the ongoing war on Al Qaeda, although compared to the State Department annuals (above) they are less illuminating on other anti-terrorism initiatives.

*Paul Wilkinson. Terrorism versus Democracy: The Liberal State Response.*
London: Routledge, 2011.
Now in its third and final edition, this has been perhaps the best single textbook for collegiate classes. Dr. Wilkinson was a founder of terrorism studies and co-editor of a strong book series in the field, started by Frank Cass Publishers and continued by Routledge/Taylor & Francis.

# INDEX